The Early Modern Englishwoman:
A Facsimile Library of Essential Works

Part 1: Printed Writings, 1500–1640

Volume 7

Alice Sutcliffe

The Early Modern Englishwoman:
A Facsimile Library of Essential Works

Part 1: Printed Writings, 1500–1640

Volume 7

Alice Sutcliffe

Selected and Introduced by
Patrick Cullen

General Editors
Betty S. Travitsky and Patrick Cullen

Published by
SCOLAR PRESS
Gower House
Croft Road
Aldershot
Hants GU11 3HR
England

Ashgate Publishing Company
Old Post Road
Brookfield
Vermont 05036-9704
USA

British Library Cataloguing-in-Publication data.

Early Modern Englishwoman: Facsimile Library of Essential Works. – Part 1: Printed Writings, 1500–1640. – Vol. 7: "Meditations of Man's Mortalitie" by A. Sutcliffe. – facsim. of 1634 ed
   828.408

Library of Congress Cataloging-in-Publication data.

The early modern Englishwoman: a facsimile library of essential works. Part 1. Printed writings, 1500–1640 / general editors, Betty S. Travitsky and Patrick Cullen.

See page vi for complete CIP Block 95-20837

The woodcut reproduced on the title page and on the case is from the title page of Margaret Roper's translation of Erasmus's *A Devout Treatise upon the Pater Noster* (circa 1524).

ISBN 1 85928 098 6

Printed in Great Britain by Antony Rowe Ltd, Chippenham

CONTENTS

Library of Congress Cataloging-in-Publication Data

The early modern Englishwoman : a facsimile library of essential
  works. Part 1. Printed writings, 1500–1640 / general editors,
  Betty S. Travitsky & Patrick Cullen.
    Contents: v. 1. Anne Askew / intro. J.N. King –
  v. 2. Works by and attributed to Elizabeth Cary / intro.
  M.W. Ferguson – v. 3. Katherine Parr / intro. J. Mueller –
  v. 4. Defences of Women, Jane Anger, Rachel Sowernam,
  and Constantia Munda / intro. S.G. O'Malley – v. 5.
  Admirable events / S. DuVerger / intro. J. Collins – v. 6.
  M. Sidney Herbert, A discourse of life and death / intro.
  G. Waller – v. 7. Alice Sutcliffe / intro. P. Cullen – v. 8.
  Margaret Tyler / intro. K. Coad – v. 9. Anne Wheathill /
  intro. P. Cullen – v. 10. Mary Wroth / intro. J.A. Roberts.
  ISBN 1-85928-226-1 (set) – ISBN 1-85928-092-7 (v. 1) –
  ISBN 1-85928-093-5 (v. 2) – ISBN 1-85928-094-3 (v. 3) –
  ISBN 1-85928-095-1 (v. 4) – ISBN 1-85928-096-X (v. 5) –
  ISBN 1-85928-097-8 (v. 6) – ISBN 1-85928-098-6 (v. 7) –
  ISBN 1-85928-099-4 (v. 8) – ISBN 1-85928-100-1 (v. 9) –
  ISBN 1-85928-101-X (v. 10)
    1. English literature—Early modern, 1500–1700.
  2. Women—England—History—Renaissance,
  1450–1600—Sources.   3. Women—England—History
  —17th century—Sources.   4. English literature—Women
  authors.   5. Women—Literary collections.   6. Women—
  England—Biography.
  I. Travitsky, Betty S.   II. Cullen, Patrick.
  PR1121.E19   1995
  820.8′ 09287′ 09031—dc20
                                        95-20837
                                        CIP

PREFACE
BY THE GENERAL EDITORS

Until very recently, scholars of the early modern period have assumed that there were no Judith Shakespeares in early modern England. Much of the energy of the current generation of scholars has been devoted to constructing a history of early modern England that takes into account what women actually wrote, what women actually read, and what women actually did. In so doing the masculinist representation of early modern women, both in their own time and ours, is deconstructed. The study of early modern women has thus become one of the most important – indeed perhaps the most important – means for the rewriting of early modern history.

The Early Modern Englishwoman: A Facsimile Library of Essential Works is one of the developments of this energetic reappraisal of the period. As the names on our advisory board and our list of editors testify, it has been the beneficiary of scholarship in the field and we hope it will also be an essential part of that scholarship's continuing momentum.

The Early Modern Englishwoman is designed to make available a comprehensive and focused collection of writings in English from 1500 to 1700, both by women and for and about them. The first series in the facsimile library provides a comprehensive if not entirely complete collection of the separately published writings by women. In reprinting these writings we intend to remedy one of the major obstacles to the advancement of feminist criticism of the early modern period, namely the unavailability of the very texts upon which the field is based. The volumes in the facsimile library reproduce carefully chosen copies of these texts, incorporating significant variants (usually in appendices). Each text is preceded by a short introduction providing an overview of the life and work of the writer along with a survey of important scholarship. These works, we strongly believe, deserve a large readership – of historians, literary critics, feminist critics, and non-specialist readers.

The Early Modern Englishwoman: A Facsimile Library of Essential Works is published in two parts: *Printed Writings, 1500–1640* and *Printed Writings, 1641–1700*. We project that it will be complemented by separate facsimile series of *Essential Works for the Study of Early Modern Women* and of *Manuscript Writings*, and by a series of original monographs on early modern gender studies, also under our general editorship.

New York City
1996

INTRODUCTORY NOTE

Virtually everything we know about Alice Sutcliffe is the result of the research of Ruth Hughey and Jeslyn Medoff (Greer 90–93). About her life little is known, not even the dates of her birth and death. We do know that she was the daughter of Luke Woodhouse of Kimberly, Norfolk, who was of the family of Sir Thomas Woodhouse, attendant to Prince Henry in the court of James I (Greer 90); but we do not know the name of her mother. By 1624 she was married to John Sutcliffe, who was 'Esquire to the body of James I' (*Harleian MS 1052*, quoted by Hughey 161). He was also nephew of Dr. Matthew Sutcliffe (1550?–1629), who was the Dean of Exeter, a chaplain in the court of James I (1603–25), and the founder of an anti-Catholic polemical college at Chelsea (*DNB*). By the time of publication of 'The Second Edition, enlarged' of the *Meditations of Man's Mortalitie, or, A Way to True Blessednesse* in 1634, John Sutcliffe had become, so the title page informs us, 'Groome of his Maiesties [i.e., Charles I (1625–49)] most Honourable Privie Chamber'. 'The Epistle Dedicatorie', addressed to Catherine Villiers (widow of George Villiers, first Duke of Buckingham, to whom John Sutcliffe may have been a servant) and to Susan(na) Villiers (Buckingham's sister and hence Catherine's sister-in-law, also wife of the Earl of Denbigh), suggests that Alice had a role at court that went beyond her being the wife of John Sutcliffe:

... and for that you [i.e., Catherine] have beene more then a *Mother* to mee, I having onely from her received life, but next under God from your Grace, & your honorable *Sister* [i.e., Susan] she being both of mee and mine [perhaps a reference to Alice's only known child, also named Susan]. By which as there is none greater then your *Selfe* to whom in duty I am bound, so there is not any to whom I with greater Prosperity both for *Temporall* and *Sprituall* blessings, then to your Grace ...

The exact nature of Alice's relationship to these two important women in the court of Charles II is never specified, but a certain warmth, if not intimacy, is suggested by her words. Perhaps she was, or had been, a member of the household of one of them; perhaps, so Ruth Hughey (160, n.2) speculates, the Duchess of Buckingham had arranged for Alice's marriage with John Sutcliffe, 'for the Duke of Buckingham in 1627 has an "ancient servant", John Sutcliffe, who was doubtless related to the younger Sutcliffe (*Calendar of State Papers Domestic*, Charles I, 1627–1628, p. 491)'. However, as Jeslyn Medoff has suggested to me, this conjecture is made somewhat less than inevitable when one remembers that 'ancient' can bear its older meaning of 'longstanding', and may possibly have its Latin sense of 'former', so the 'ancient servant' referred to in *CSPD* may be Alice's husband. Whichever reading one accepts of the passage in *CPSD*, it would seem clear the Sutcliffes had, directly or indirectly, a fairly longstanding connection with the Duchess of Buckingham that extended back before the assassination of the Duke in 1628.

The '*Spirituall*' dimension of Sutcliffe's *Meditations* is framed by a distinctly '*Temporall*' dimension: very much like Aemelia Lanier's elaborately encomiastic volume *Salve Deus Rex Judaeorum* ('Written by Mistress Aemilia Lanyer, Wife to Captaine Alfonso Lanyer, Servant to the Kings Majestie'), her volume ('Written by Mrs. Alice Sutcliffe, wife of John Sutcliffe, Esquire, Groome of his Majesties most Honourable Privie Chamber') is clearly designed, in its dedications and encomia, to promote her husband and herself. As noted above, the dedicatory epistle is addressed to two of the most powerful women in the Caroline court, and it is followed by three acrostic encomia. The first two encomia are to the joint dedicatees; the third is to Philip, Earl of Pembroke and Montgomery, who, as Lord Chamberlain of the Household, was her husband's superior. The testimonial poems from Ben Jonson, Thomas May, George Withers, Peter Heywood, and Francis Lenton also reflect the Sutcliffes' efforts to make her volume into a court event. All of these, Heywood excepted, were prominent writers in the Caroline court, and at least one of them, Withers, was apparently solicited to write a testimonial by Alice's husband: Withers addresses his poem 'To Mr. John Sutcliffe, Esq. upon the receipt of this Book written by his Wife', and he begins, 'Sir, I receiv'd your Booke with acceptation, / and thus returne a due congratulation'.

Meditations of Man's Mortalitie consists of six prose meditations followed by a long poem of eighty-eight six-line stanzas (ababcc) on 'our losse by Adam, and our gayne by Christ'. In this period, the term 'meditation' covers a wide range of forms, from Donne's *Devotions* to Henry Colman's *Divine Meditations*. As Barbara Lewalski (83) has argued, for Protestants there is a 'near-identification of sermon and meditation'. Certainly Sutcliffe's meditations read like sermons, with their strings of biblical quotations and paraphrases connected by moral and exegetical reflection. At the same time, Sutcliffe makes a fairly sustained effort, usually at the beginning of each meditation, to link each of the prose sections into a unifying argument, suggested in the subtitle, of 'A Way to True Blessednesse' by our acceptance, first, of our mortality and wickedness and then of God's mercy. The claim in the table of contents that her work is a 'treatise' is thus not entirely off the mark.

The poem, while it occupies almost a third of the volume, is not mentioned on the title page or in the table of contents; and although its religious subject matter links it to the prose meditations, it is not entirely clear whether the poem is designed as a coda to the meditations or as a separate work. One possible connection between the two sections is a numerological structure based on sixes and sevens: the six meditations in prose can be viewed as being completed by a seventh section in poetry that is itself composed of sixes (the sixaines). Be that as it may, the poem clearly proceeds according to the same spiritual 'way to true blessedness' of the prose treatise, that is, it begins as a meditation on the corruption of our fallen nature and progresses to a meditation on the blessedness obtainable through Christ's sacrifice. It also contains the volume's longest development of one traditional technique of meditation, *compositio loci* (composition of the place), in which the meditator treats a major biblical event as though it were occurring in the present and often addresses one of the participants in that event (Martz 25–32). For Sutcliffe, this event is the Fall, and in what may be for many readers the most interesting section of her work, she devotes the first pages of her poem to an address to (and rebuke of) Eve.

The title page of *Meditations* suggests that it went through two editions. There is an entry in the Stationers' Register (30 January 1632/33) made to 'Master Seile' for what apparently was the first edition:

> Entred for his Copy vnder the hands of master Buckner and master Aspley warden a booke called *Meditacions of Mans mortallity or a way to true blessednes &c* by Alice Sutcliffe. . . .

No copies of this edition survive. We reprint 'the Second Edition, enlarged' in this facsimile edition. Exactly what the enlargement consists of we cannot say. Hughey (156–57) speculates that the enlargement refers to the testimonial verses, but it could also refer to the poem: the fact that the poem is mentioned neither on the title page nor in the table of contents may reflect its status as an addition to the original work.

Only four copies survive of the second edition (at The British Library, Peterborough Cathedral, The Huntington Library, and the Folger Shakespeare Library); it is a duodecimo volume (text block 7 cm. × 12.1 cm.). We have chosen the Folger copy of the second edition as the most readable of existing copies, although illegible lines on pages 179 and 180 have been patched from The British Library copy. Bernard Alsop and Thomas Fawcett, the printers responsible for this volume, were noted for producing books that are 'very poor specimens of typography' (Plomer 4). Alsop's printing materials were transferred to him from his first partner, Thomas Creed; they dated back to 1580 and were already in bad condition when they came into Alsop's hands, but he used them for the rest of his career. The appearance of this volume notwithstanding, Alsop and his partner Fawcett were not unimportant printers (they published much of the dramatic literature of Beaumont and Fletcher, Dekker, Greene, and others; and Alsop was one of the twenty master printers allowed by the Act of 1637).

References

STC 23447

Greer, Germaine et al. (ed.), (1988), *Kissing the Rod: An Anthology of Seventeenth-Century Women's Verse*, London: Virago

Hughey, Ruth (1934), 'Forgotten Verses by Ben Jonson, George Wither, and Others to Alice Sutcliffe', *RES*, 10, 156–64

Lewalski, Barbara Kiefer (1973), *Donne's 'Anniversaries' and the Poetry of Praise*, Princeton: Princeton University Press

Martz, Louis (1954), *The Poetry of Meditation*, New Haven: Yale University Press

Plomer, Henry R. (1907), *A Dictionary of Booksellers and Printers Who Were at Work in England, Scotland and Ireland from 1641 to 1667*, London: The Bibliographical Society

PATRICK CULLEN

Meditations of Man's Mortalitie (STC 23447) is reproduced, by permission, from the copy at the Folger Shakespeare Library. The text block of the copy measures 7 × 12.1 cm.

St Lovu

Marg e Mânoa

Meditations

OF

M A N'S

MORTALITIE.

OR,

A WAY TO TRVE

Blessednesse.

WRITTEN,
By Mrs. ALICE SVTCLIFFE
wife of *Iohn Sutcliffe* Esquire,
Groome of his Maiesties
most Honourable Priuie
Chamber.
The Second EDITION, enlarged.

ROM. 6.
*The wages of sinne is Death, but the
guift of GOD, is Eternall life,
through* IESVS CHRIST *our Lord.*

LONDON
Printed by *B. A.* and *T. F.* for
Henry Seyle at the *Tygers* head
in *Pauls* Church-yard. 1634.

TO

THE MOST

ILLVSTRIOVS

AND

GRACIOVS

PRINCESSE,

KATHERINE

DVTCHESSE

OF

BVCKINGHAM:

A 3   AND

AND
THE RIGHT
HONOVRABLE
AND
VERTVOVS
LADY,
SVSANNA,
COVNTESSE
OF
DENBEIGH
her Sister.

Graci-

Gracious Prin-cesse :

WHen I read how the Gods sooner accepted of a Handfull of *Frankensence* offered by pure *Devotion*, then whole Hecatombes of *Arabian* Spices in *Ostentation* : I am incouraged, having duely conside-

A 4   red

red Your unlimited
Goodnesse, to present
this my Mite unto
your *Grace*, and your
Honourable *Sister*, For
as you are Twinnes in
Virtues, so I have joy-
ned You in my *Devoti-*
ons : Where first, I most
humbly crave of You
to passe a favourable
Censure of my procee-
dings, it beeing, I know
not usuall for a *Woman*
to doe such things :
Yet ELIHA sayth,
There is a Spirit in Man,
and the inspiration of the
Almightie giveth them
Vnder-

Vnderstanding. And it is sayd againe : *Out of the mouthes of Babes and Sucklings, thou shalt perfect Praise.* I am assured, I shall meet with mocking *Ishmaels*, that will carpe at *Goodnesse*; wherefore, I runne to Your selues for *refuge*; humbly craving to bee assisted by your *Graciousnesse*, which will appeare as the Splendant *Sunne* to disperse those *Mists.* I have chosen a *subiect* not altogether *Pleasing*; but my ayme is,

is, that it may prove *Profitable*, having ob-
served in this short
course of my Pilgri-
mage, how apt *Man*
is, not to thinke of his
Mortalitie, which
stealeth upon him as a
Thiefe in the night: Experience teacheth mee,
that there is no *Acti-
on* wisely undertaken,
whereof the *End* is not
fore-casted, in the first
place, howsoever it bee
last put in execution; I
have ever accompted
Ingratitude, to be like

a

a *Beast*, who having received *benefites*, thinkes not of any *acknowledgements*. Owing therefore, a due Debt of *Thankefulneſſe* for Your unexpreſſable undeſerved *Favours*, and being no wayes able to cauſe the deſires of my Heart to appeare *worthy*-your *Acceptances*, I have made choyſe of this, as being perſwaded thereto, by that truely Noble vertuouſnes which hath evidently appeared in You, to the ſtrengthening

ning of *Goodnesse*, that
heere it may find *admittance*, which otherwise
might want *Entertainement*; and for that you
have beene more then
a *Mother* to mee, I having onely from her received life, but next
under God from your
Grace, & your honorable *Sister* the being both
of mee and mine. By
which as there is none
greater then your *Selfe*
to whom in duty I am
bound, so there is not
any to whom I wish
greater Prosperity both
for

for *Temporall* and *Spiri-tuall* blessings, then to your Grace; beseech-ing God to preserve you and your Honora-ble Off-spring here up-on Earth, with my no lesse vertuous Lady your *Sister*, to whom I am tyed by the same bonds of *Thankfulnesse*, that as God hath made your *Renownes* great up-on earth, so I beseech him to adde to your *Lives* length of dayes, and after life, Eternall happinesse in the Hea-vens,

vens, whither CHRIST is gone to prepare a place for You, I alwayes remayning,

Your Graces,

and your Honors

truely devoted

Servant,

Alice Sutcliffe.

AN

AN
ACCROSTIQVE,

Upon the Renowned
Name of the most vertuous
Princesse, KATHERINE
Dutchesse of Buc-
kingham.
(*ₓ*)

K Now

KNow you this Princesse, B v c-
KINGHAM's Chast Dutchesse?
ASke aged Time with his worm-
eaten Crutches,
TO find amongst the numbers of
his Role
HEr Paralell, of such a Heavenly
moule,
EXcelling so i'th' beauties of the
Soule:
RIch in all Treasures, that to Vir-
tue tend:
IN Faith, Hope, Charity; the bles-
sed's end.
NOr is there ought, that lives in
Woman kinde:
EXceeding the rare prowesse of
her Minde.

Borne

BOrne of High blood, from Rvt-
                LANDS Family :

VNited to a Duke of Royall
                   state.

CVrs'd bee the time, more curs'd
                 his cruelty

KIll'd him ; and reav'd this Turtle
                 of her mate,

IN peerlesse woe, we still lament
                 that fate :

NOr shall his memorie e're out of
                 date.

GOe on then Gracious Princesse,
                 grac't by Fame,

HOnour shall still, attend your no-
                 ble Name :

ANd as your Goodnesse hath a-
                 bounded, so

MAy Heaven the greatest good
                 on Youbestow.

AN ACCROSTIQVE,

Vpon the Name of the Right
Honourable, and truely vertuous
Lady; *SVSANNA*, Countesse
of *Denbigh*.

SEe heere a Lady, blessed in her
                                    birth,

VNto whose Greatnesse, Goodnes
                            ioyn'd is still :

SVSANNA ne're so famous was
                                    on Earth

AS is this Lady, lead by vertuous
                                        will,

NOthing so sweete to her, as hea-
                                venly mirth,

NO Musike sounds like *Halelviah*
                                        still,

A Happy Soule, which those de-
                        lights doth fill.
                                    Daigne

Daigne then to view these lines,
  where truely I
Expresse but truth, not vsing Flat-
  tery:
NO Fallaces within my mouth
  once lurkes,
BVt hates all those, that use dissem-
  bling workes.
EVen as your Goodnesse merits, so
  speake I
I Am your Servant, bound vntill I
  dye:
GIve leave, then gracious Lady, for
  I finde,
HEaven hath indu'd you, with a
  vertuous minde.

AN ACCROSTIQVE,

*Vpon the name and Titles of the
Right honourable and my ever
honored Lord, PHILIP Earle
of Pembroke and Montgomery,
Lord Chamberlaine of his
Majesties Houshold,
&c.*

PEMBROOKE's great Peere, your
                    Princely favour I
HEere humbly crave, to guerdon
                    my weake pen,
IF this doth show my imbeci-
                    litie,
LIke a good Patron, shroud it
                    from bad men ;
I By your favours mov'd doe
                    this present,
PRay then my Lord, accept my
                    good intent.
                          Poore

P Oore are my weake endeavours,
　　　　　　yet if you,

E Ncourage my *Minervaes*
　　　　　　infant Muse

M Y cherisht thoughts, by that,
　　　　　　may frame anew

B Ooke of true thanks, unto your
　　　　　　Lordships use :

R Ight Noble then, view but the
　　　　　　vertueus tract,

O F this small Volume, and if
　　　　　　you shall finde,

O Vght good expressed, by our
　　　　　　Sexes act,

K Now honor'd Lord, my starres
　　　　　　are very kinde.

　　　　　a ₃　　　Mountgo-

M OVNTGOMERY, my Cælique
Muſe doth mount

O N Cherubs wing, from this
low Orbe to heaven,

V Ertue'is here expreſt, vices
account;

N Or is't a Tale, or Fable that is
given

T Ruth never is aſham'd to ſhew
it's face:

G Reat man and good, but
alwayes loves the light.

O May it then, find an accepted
Grace

M Ore cauſe a woman, did the
ſame indite,

E Ven then as DEBORAH's
ſweet tuned ſong,
——— Rung

R Vng out her sacred Peale, in
holy Writ:

O So, I pray my heart, my pen,
my tongue,

Y Ea all my faculties, may
follow it:

Your Lordships

Devoted Servant,

Alice Sutcliffe.

TO
Mrs. *Alice Sutcliffe*, on her divine Meditations.

WHen I had read
your holy Meditatiõs,
And in them view'd
th' uncertainty of Life,
The motives, and true Spurres
to all good Nations.
The Peace of Conscience,
and the Godly's strife,
The Danger of delaying
to Repent,
And the deceipt of pleasures,
by Consent.

The

The côfort of weake Chriſtiās,
  with their warning,
From fearefull back-ſlides;
  And the debt we' are in,
To follow Goodneſſe,
  by our owne diſcerning
Our great reward,
  th' æternall Crown *to win.*
I ſayd, who' had ſupp'd ſo deepe
  of this ſweet Chalice,
Muſt CELIA *bee,*
  the Anagram *of* ALICE,

      Ben. Ionſon.

Vpon the Religious Meditations of Mrs. ALICE SVTCLIFFE.

TO THE READER.

Would'st thou
 (fraile Reader) thy
  true Nature see?
Behold this Glasse
 of thy Mortality.
Digest the precepts
 of this pious Booke,
Thou canst not in
 a nobler Mirrour looke.
Though sad it seeme,
 and may loose mirth destroy,
  That

That is not sad
    whish leades to perfe&t ioy.
Thanke her faire Soule
    whose meditation makes
Thee see thy frailtie ;
    nor disdaine to take
That knowledge, which
    a Womans skill can bring.
All are not Syren-notes
    that women sing.
How true that Sexe can write,
    how grave, how well,
Let all the Muses,
    and the Graces tell.

THO: MAY.

To Mr. IOHN SVTCLIFFE
Esq. upon the receipt of this
Booke written by his Wife.

S'Ir, I receiv'd your Booke
    with acceptation,
  And, thus returne
    a due congratulation,
For that good Fortune,
    which hath blest your life
By making you
    the *Spouse* of such a *Wife.*
Although I neuer saw her,
    yet I see,
The *Fruit,* and by the *Fruit*
    I judge the *Tree.*
My Praise addes nothing to it:
    That which is
Well done, can praise it selfe;
    and so may this.   (me.
To be a woman, 'tis enough with
To merit praise ;
    For I can never be   So

So much their *Friend*,
    as they have heretofore
Deserv'd; although
    they merited no more.
When, therefore
    to their *Woman-hood* I finde
The love of sacred
    Piety conioyn'd,
Me thinks I have
    my duty much forgot;
Vnlesse I praise
    (although I know them not).
But, when to *Woman-hood*
    and good *Affections*,
Those rare *Abilities*,
    and those *Perfections*,
Vnited are,
    to which our *Sexe* aspire,
Then, forc'd I am
    to *Love*, and to *admire*.
I am not of their mind,
    who if they see,

                        Some

Some *Female-Studies*
    fairely ripened be,
(With Masculine successe)
    doe peevishly,
Their worths due honour
    unto them deny,
By overstrictly
    censuring the same;
Or doubting whether
    from themselves it came,
For, well I know,
    Dame *Pallas* and the *Muses*,
Into that *Sexe*,
    their faculties infuses,
As freely as to *Men*;
    and they that know,
How to improve their *Guift*,
    shall find it so.
Then ioy in your good *Lot*,
    and praises due
To *Him* ascribe, that thus
    hath honor'd you.
                    Geo. Withers.

Vpon the Meditations of M^{rs}. ALICE SVTCLIFFE.

I Have no Muse my owne,
    but what I see
Worthy of praise,
    that is a Muse to me.
Divinity (the highest theame)
    will find
No fitter subiect
    then an humble mind,
And as in scorne of them
    that are more fit
By Instruments lesse notable
    expresseth it.
Almes and Deuotion,
    Zeale and Charity.
Might for thy Sexe
    beseeming Scripture be,
But when thou speak'st
    of death, and that iust doome

Which

Which shall on all
  conditions, ages, come,
And thence descending
  to Philosophie,
Teachest weake Nature
  how to learne to dye:
It seemes to me
  above thy Sex and State,
Some heavenly sparke
  doth thee illuminate.
Live still a praise,
  but no example to
Others, to hope,
  as thou hast done, to doe.
Live still thy sexes honour,
  and when Death
(With whō thou art acquainted)
  stoppes thy breath
Fame to Posteritie
  shall make thee shine
And adde thy Name
  vnto the Muses nine.

PET: HEYVVOOD.

AN
ENCOMIVM
vpon the Authoresse
and Booke.

Great Ladies that to *vertue*
    are inclin'd,
    See here the pious practice
    of a wife,
Expressed by the beauties
    of the Mind,
And now set forth
    in Pictures of the life;
        Wherein

Wherein matter and forme
    are both at strife
Who shall be Master :
    but i'th end hands shooke,
For that they haue
    a Mistresse to theyr Booke.

Whose Language I must needs
    (in truth) admire,
And how such Elegance
    should from her spring :
Vntill I thinke of Zeale
    (that Calique fire)
Which might transport her soule,
    by Cherubs wing
In Prose or Numbers,
    piously to sing
Precepts of Praise,
    worthy your approbation ;
               For

For she is Rara Avis
   in our Nation.

And though her youth,
   gives her no SYBILS *name*
Nor doth she Prophecie,
   as they of old :
Yet she's indu'd
   with the most sacred flame
Of Poesie Divine ;
   and doth unfold
Nought but the truth,
   and therefore may be bold.
Whose holy paines,
   and study here exprest,
Shall Register her name
   amongst the blest.
VRANIA,
   is her most heavenly Muse.
                              Which

Which flyeth vpwards,
    where her minde is placed.
She sings such Songs,
    as DEBORAH did vse.
When she, and BARVCH
    had their foes abased;
For which, with Lawrell
    shee may well be graced.
And stil'd the Paragon,
    of these our Times,
In her sweet Prose,
    and true composed Rimes.

But thinke not Ladies
    that I doe contriue,
Numbers to mend
    ought that is done amisse;
Or that I meane,
    to keepe her name aliue
                     When

When she is gone :
    and pass'd to greater blisse,
For I ne're knew her,
    when I framed this.
Onely I read her lines,
    which forc't me praise
The Picture of her minde,
    with this course bayes.

FRA: LENTON

THE

THE
Contents of the en-
suing Treatise.

I.

VVHerde the uncer-
tainty of *Mans*
life expressed, and of the
fearefull end of the Wic-
ked.   *Fol.* 1.

II.

*Motines and Inducements
to true Godlinesse.*
              Fol. 5 3.

III.

*Of the Peace of a good
Conscience, and the Joy-
full*

full end of the godly.

MEDI.

MEDITATIONS
OF MANS
Mortality.

I.

Wherein the uncertainty of Mans life is expressed, and of the fearefull end of the Wicked.

Hen I behold the Heavens & the earth, the workemanship of the Almighty, and see in it all Creatures both for

B   com-

Psalm.8.

commodity and pleasure, which as a store-house, preserue all things for the behoofe and benefit of Man: I cannot but vse to my selfe, the saying of the Prophet D A V I D; Lord! what is Man, that thou shouldest thinke on him; or the Sonne of man, that thou shouldest be mindfull of him, thou hast made him but a little lower then the Angels; thou hast crowned him with honour and worship; by reason of which, I thinke him to be onely happy, and a God vpon earth; and that there is no blessednes beyond this: but looking into him with more deliberation, I find his

his breath is in his noſtrils, and that hee is as the Beaſt that periſheth; I find his life to be but a ſpan, and the perpetuity of his Happineſſe, no better then a Flower, which flouriſheth to day, and to morrow is cut downe and withereth; and that his habitation is but a Pilgrimage, hee hath no certaine abiding, I perceiue there is no building of Tabernacles heere, this is no place of reſt. I remember the Foole, that ſayd to his ſoule, There was much laid vp for many yeares, but that night his ſoule was taken from him, and how that after Death hee muſt

Eccleſ.3.

Luke,12.

B 2 giue

give an account of his Stewardſhip, for they are not his, but lent him of the Lord; neyther to abuſe through exceſſe, nor niggerdice, but to put them foorth to the beſt vſe, and to the glory of him who is the giver of all good things.

For it is true, that a Philoſopher ſayth; Hee that ſeeketh for true Happines in this world, followeth a ſhaddow, which when hee thinketh hee is ſureſt of, vaniſheth and is nothing; and the Apoſtle P A V L ſayth; If in this life wee were onely happie, wee were of all men moſt miſerable.

Seeing

Seeing then it is so, That man which is borne of a woman hath but a short time to liue, and that few and euill are the dayes of his Pilgrimage, pointed out but to Threescore and tenne, and if Nature befriend him so farre, as to affoord him life till Foure score, yet is it so full of infirmities, that it becomes a burthen to him, Life being a brittle and miserable fetter, which chaineth the pure and everlasting soule, to the vile, sinfull, and corruptible body. *Iob. 14.*

Yet where is hee, that takes the Wise mans counsell, To remember his Creator, in the dayes of *Eccles. 12.*

B 3   his

his Youth, before the e-
vill day comes, and the
time approach, in the
which, he shall say; I have
no pleasure in them; for if
a man live many yeares
and rejoyce in them all,
yet let him remember the
dayes of Darknes, for they
are many; the Sun sets and
riseth againe; but thou a-
las, when thy glasse is run,
and the short gleame of
thy Summers Sun is spent,
shall never returne againe.
How soone alas, is thy span
grasped, thy minute wa-
sted, thy flower dead, thy
vapor of life gone; with-
out thought, without
dread, eyther of sinnes past,
or ascompts to come?
Where

Where is there one, that lookes into the estate of his Soule, with a serious eye; that examines his conscience, unvayleth his heart, and considereth his wayes, and how that he is every day of his life, a dayes journey nearer his end; and nothing is wanting for the expiration thereof, but the stroke of death, which commeth in a moment; and then thou art gone, eyther to unexpressable endlesse Ioyes, or easelesse and endlesse miseries. For no sooner art thou borne to possesse this World, but death issueth forth incontinently out of his Sepulcher, to finde thy life; ney-

B 4　　　　　　ther

ther doth he alwayes send his harbinger before, to acquaint thee with his comming, but many times entreth unexpected, unlooked for ; and yet darest thou rest in security; me thinkes it should make thee tremble, were not thy conscience seared; to think of the divinenesse of that Iustice, before whom, thou art to stand, being in the day of his Wrath, and at the barre of his Iudgment: canst thou thinke then, to bee able to indure his angry eye, whose sight will pierce to the very centure of thy heart and soule, and rip up every festred corner of thy conscience?

ence ? O then ! bethinke
thy felfe in time, before
that gloomy day comes,
that day of Cloudes and
thicke darkeneffe, that day
of defolation and confufion
approach ; when all the
Inhabitants of the Earth
fhall mourne and lament,
and all faces fhall gather
blackneff . Becaufe, the
time of their Iudgement
is come ; alas! with what a
tearefull hart and weeping
eyes, and forrowfull countenance, & trebling loynes,
wilt thou at that laft and
great affize looke upon
CHRIST IESVS, when he
fhall moft glorioufly ap-
peare, with innumerable
Angels in flaming fire, to

B 5   render

Ioel. 2.

render vengeance on them
that know him not? What
a cold dampe will seaze
upon thy soule, when
thou shalt behold him,
whom thou hast all thy life
long, reiected in his ordi-
nances, despised in his
members, and neglected in
his love: what horror and
terror of spirit will possesse
thee; how wilt thou cry
to the Rockes and Moun-
taines to fall upon thee, and
cover thee from the fierce-
nes of his Wrath ; when
thou shalt behold, the Hea-
vens burning, the Elements
melting, the Earth trem-
bling, the Sea roaring, the
Sunne turne into darknes,
and the Moone into bloud:
how

how will thy numberlesse
sinnes in hideous formes
appeare before thee, every
one of them bearing the
Ensignes of Gods heavie
displeasure , dipped in a
bloudy coloured dye ; and
crying out, for vengeance
against thee : alas ! if thy
faultring tongue should go
about to faine some see-
ming shew of a colcurable
excuse, how soone would
it be stopped, all thy actions both for thoughts ,
words, and deeds, being
registred in a booke , and
kept within the Court of
Heaven. Oh remember
how terrible his voyce was
when he gave his Law to
his chosen people, and thinkest

kest thou, it will bee lesse
terrible, when he shall de-
mand an account of that
Law, which thou hast so
many times carelesly bro-
ken. Oh then, whither will
his wrath cary thee, whither
will the blast of his breath
hurry thee; it was thy sins
that inflamed his wrath, &
his wrath will inflame that
fire which will never goe
out : Oh then alas, whil'st
thou hast time, become thy
own friend, looke into thy
selfe, and by a serious exa-
mination, prove the Pilot
of thy owne Ship , which
now lyeth floating on the
Seas of this troublesome
World, ballanc'd onely
with cares, and disquieting
pleasures of this life , and
how

how thou saylest with a full course, towards the haven of endlesse Happines ; yet one blast of unprepared death will turne thy sayles, and plunge thee irrecoverably into that bottomlesse Gulfe , where one houres torment, will infinitely exceed all the pleasures thy whole life contained : and wilt thou now standing upon the very brim of Hell, melt in thy delights : Alas, slippery is thy footing, and thy hold but by the thread of life, which stretched to the length, soone crackes : yet how triflingly spendest thou thy pretious time, tyring out thy spirits, and robbing thine eyes of their beloved

beloved sleepe, for those things, to the which, the time will come,that the very remembrance of them will be bitter, and to the which,thou must bid an everlasting farewell.

Yet not considering these things? how many are there,that only spend their time in jollity,and sodainly goe downe to the Grave; they cry to themselves; Peace, peace, when sodaine Destruction overtakes them, not once thinking of IEREMIA'S lamentation for *Ierusalem*; wherein hee complaines, *Lamen.1.* That shee remembred not her last end.

Would they but consider,

der, that as the Tree fal-
leth ſo it lyeth ; and as
Death leaves them, ſo ſhall
Iudgement finde them ;
they would not draw Ini-
quity with cords of vani-
ty, nor ſinne as with cart-
ropes ; did they thinke
upon the reward of Sinne;
did they conſider how full
of griefe and miſery, how
ſhort and tranſitorious
this preſent life is, and the
vaine Pleaſures thereof:
how on every ſide, theyr
enemies compaſſe them,
and that Death lyeth in
wayte againſt them, every
where catching them ſo-
dainly and unawares. Did
that ſaying often ſound in
theyr eares, *Ariſt and*
come

come to Judgement, they would not deferre theyr Repentance to theyr laſt end, or their old-age; when it can not be ſayd, that they leave Sin, but ſinne them. Shall they offer to the Divell, the World, and their owne fleſh, the flower and ſtrength of theyr yeares, and ſerve God with the lees and dregs : when the Prophet MALACHY complayned of the peoples evill Offerings, hee ſayd; Offer it now unto thy Governour, will hee be pleaſed with thee, or accept thy perſon : and can they thinke, this great GOD will bee pleaſed with them. If RABSHE-CHA

Mal. 1.

2. King. 18

CHA and HOLOFERNES,
but Meſſengers for theyr
Lords, tooke it ſo ill; that
the Iewes came not forth
to make theyr peace with
them, that they threatned
nothing ſhould pacifie
their furie, but theyr De-
ſtruction : How much
more, ſhall this King of
Kings, and Lord of Lords,
whoſe wrath is ſo kindled
for theyr wickedneſſe,
condemne them into ut-
ter Darkneſſe, where ſhall
bee wayling and gnaſhing
of teeth, (for no dead car-
rion ſo lothſomly ſtinketh
in the noſtrils of an earthly man, as doth the wic-
ked, abhominable unre-
pentant man, in the pre-
ſence

Iudith. 5.

sence of God;) yet not
considering this, they goe
on in a carelesse security,
heaping one sinne upon
another, till the burthen
become unsupportable, and
the vials of Gods wrath
ready to bee powred on
them, not once calling
them, to theyr remem-
brance; or if they doe, it is
so farre from Contrition,
that it is rather a delight
to them, often glorying in
the often cōmittings ther-
of; they neyther thinking
of theyr account, nor their
end, wherein yet they
might haue some happines;
if death were the dissolving
both of their body & soule.

For being rid of their
bodies,

bodies, they should also be rid of theyr Soules and Sinnes : But forasmuch, as it is evident, that the Soule is immortall, there is left no comfort for the wicked to trust in. Therfore, let such remember Esav , Who hauing once rejected the Blessing, could not after obtayne it, though he sought it with teares; when it is too late, with the fiue Foolish Virgins, they may cry; Lord, Lord, open to vs; but the gates of Mercy will bee shut, and it will be answered, *I know you not.*

Then woe bee to the sinfull wicked men , that haue not power to turne from

Gen. 27.

Math. 25

from the filthy workes of
this finfull and wretched
World, that hindereth
them from the blissfull
state, and keepeth backe
theyr Soules from the presence of God : For when
Gods Serjeant Death, shall
arrest them, and they shall
bee summon'd to appeare
before the Tribunall of
the Almighty, with what
terrible feare will that
Soule be shaken and smit-
ten, and with how many
speares of a piercing Conscience, is hee gored and
thrust through; he will then
begin to thinke of the
time past, present, and that
to come: The time past, he
may behold with asto-
nishment

nishment, to perceiue how
fast it fleeted, and the mul-
titude of sinnes therein
committed , the which
were accounted pleasures,
but are now terrors, for e-
very one of which, he must
answere; for as saith a Philosopher : An accusing
Conscience is the secret,&
most terrible thing that
can bee, at the approaching
and comming of Death, and
infinit & vnspeakable are
the feares and griefes it
will bring with it; for then
hee will grieve, that the
time of Repentance hath
beene so ill & lewdly past,
he seeth the divine Comman-
dements which he hath
contemned ; he is afflicted,
because

becaufe he feeth the inevitable houre approach, of rendring an account, & of the divine juft vengance; he would tarry ftill, but he is conftrained to depart; he would recover that is paft, but time is not granted: if he looke behind him, he feeth the courfe and race of his whole life led, as a moment of time; if he looke before, he beholdeth the infinit fpace of Eternity which expecteth him, he forroweth and fobbeth, becaufe he hath loft the joy of euerlafting Eternity, which hee might haue obtained in fo fhort a time; hee tormenteth himfelfe, becaufe he hath

hath lost the ineffable sweetnesse of perpetuall delight, for one sensuall, carnall, and momentany pleasure; he blusheth, considering, that for that substance which is Wormes-meat, he hath dispised that which Angels prize so highly; and weighing the glory of those immortall riches, hee is confounded, that he hath changed them for the basenesse and vildenesse of Temporall things; but when he casteth his eyes upon things below, and seeth the darke and obscure valley of this world, and beholdeth above it, the shining brightnesse of eternall Light, then

then he confeſſeth, that all that he loved in this world, was blacke night and ugly darkneſſe.

To behold the time preſent, is as ill; for there hee can finde nothing, but weakeneſſe and paines; his friends eyther mourning by him, or elſe not able to ſtay with him, to ſee his torments, which in this life, God hath begun to let him taſte; having painefull Limbes, darke Eyes, a faultering Tongue, hard browes, ſhort breath, and a panting heart, haſting to appeare before God, who he muſt behold; not as his Father, but a moſt feirce Iudge, whoſe pure eyes beheld

beheld all his actions, and
that through all his life
saw nothing but wicked-
nesse, no sorrowing teares
to wash away those pollu-
tions; and therefore that
leporous life must receiue
a heauie condemnation:
there will not be any to
speake for him, neyther
will he be able to answere
one word for a thousand;
all those pleasures now
stand up to accuse him, and
his owne Conscience giues
in evidence against him,
saying to himselfe the
words of SALOMON; How   *Pro. 5.*
haue I hated instruction,
and my heart despised re-
proofe, and I haue not o-
beyed the voyce of my tea-
C   chers,

chers, nor enclined mine
eare to them that instruct-
ed me; woe is me poore
wretch, into what a labo-
rinth haue my sinnes led
me; how suddenly, and
thinking nothing lesse,
hath this houre intrapped
me, how hath it rushed vpon me, I never dreamed
of it; what doe now my
Honours profit me, what
doe now all my Dignities
helpe me, what doe all my
friends for me, what profit
doe now my servants
bring mee, what fruit doe
I now reape of all my riches and goods which I was
wont to possesse; for now
a small piece of ground of
seaven foot will concaine
me,

me, and I muft be content
with a dwelling in a nar-
row Coffin, and with a
lodging in a poore Win-
ding fheet; my riches, fhall
remaine here behind mee,
which I fcraped together
with fo great toyle, and
fweating, others fhall en-
joy them, and fhall fpend
them on theyr pleafures,
onely my finnes, which I
haue committed in gathe-
ring them, wayte upon me,
that I may fuffer deferved
punifhment for them;
what can I make now of
all my Pleafures and De-
lights, feeing they are all
over-paft, onely theyr
dregges are my Potion,
which are fcruples and
C 2   bytings

bytings of Conscience, which like Thornes doe pierce me, and runne thorough my miserable heart.

In what taking is this poore Soule; if time were now againe, with what an austere kinde of life would hee passe it, how would hee shun all those alluring Syrens, sower sauce findes he for his sweetes, and for a minute of Pleasures, must possesse a world of Woes; nay, woes without end, soone ended those delights, endlesse are those miseries.

O thou wretched man! thou that didst chose, rather to sit by the Flesh-
pots

pots of *Ægypt*, then by
induring a little weari-
some travailes , to enter
into the promised Land,
which floweth with Milk
and Honey ; See ! O see
now , what a long chayne
of Miseries, those thy short
Pleasures have wrought
thee. O thou foolish and
senceleste ! hadst thou no
respect to the death of
CHRIST, who dyed to
redeeme thee , but that by
thy sinnes,thou must anew
Crucifie him , and make
his Wounds to bleed a-
fresh ? Thou hast againe,
nayled him to the Crosse
by thy pollutions ! thou
hast againe,pierc'd his side,
not with one , but many

speares

speares of Blasphemy, and
as it were piece-meale, tea-
ring him from Heaven!
thou haſt grinded him, by
thy oppreſſions, which
thou didſt to maintaine thy
ſuperfluous delights.

It was his love, that cau-
ſed him to undergoe his
Fathers Wrath for thy
ſake; but what one ſinne,
haſt thou left for his?
Canſt thou ſay, and that
truly, that thou haſt ſpared
one diſh from thy Belly, to
feed his hungry Members;
or one Garment from thy
exceſſive apparell, to cloth
the naked; or one houres
ſleepe, to meditate on his
miſeries: a poore requi-
tall of ſuch infinite Love!
was

Was CHRIST stretched
on the Crosse, and couldest
thou recount it nothing to
stretch thy selfe vpon thy
downy Beds of sinne?
Did CHRIST suck downe
Vineger and Gall for thee,
and couldest thou without
pricke of Conscience, sur-
feit with overflowne
Boles? Was CHRIST
crowned with Thornes,
and couldest thou crowne
thy selfe with ease and
pleasure? Then now be-
hold, (O thou rich Glut-
ton!) thou, who wouldest
never cast up thine eyes to
behold the true happines,
till it was too late, and
consider what the allure-
ments of the Flesh now
C 4   profit

profit you, which you
then so much delighted
in? What is become of
your Riches? where are
your Honours? where are
your Treasures? where are
your Delights? were are
your Ioyes; the seaven
yeares of Plenty are past,
and other seaven yeares of
Dearth and scarcity are
come, which have devou-
red up all your Plenty, no
memory or footsteps being
Iob. 24. left of it. As it is in Iob,
Drought and heate, con-
sume the Snow waters; so
doth the Grave, those that
have Sinned; your Glory
is now perished, and your
Felicity is drowned in the
sea of Sorrowes, not one-
ly

ly your delights have not profited you, which you injoyed in this World; but they shall bee the causes of greater Torments : witnesse the Glutton in the Gospell, who fared deliciously every day, being in Hell; was not that member his Tongue, most tormented, which gave him the greatest delight in Sin.

Nay, speedily and unexpected, this horror rusheth upon them; for, as everlasting Felicity, doth quickly follow the Godly, in the short race of theyr Misery; so everlasting Misery, quickly followeth the ungodly, in the short race of theyr worldly Felicity.

C 5   It

It were better therefore, for a man to live poorely, being aſſured of the bliſſe of Heaven, then to be deprived thereof, though during life hee poſſeſſe all worldly riches; for intollerable, are the burthens they bring with them, ſeeing that the Scripture ſayth; Where much is given, much is againe required : beſides, the memory of the ungodly ſhall periſh, as ſaith Iob; The pitifull man, ſhall forget him, the Worme ſhall feele his ſweetneſſe, he ſhall bee no more remembred, and the Wicked ſhall bee broken like a Tree.

Iob, 24.

II.

Motives and inducements to true Godlinesse.

Having already spoken of the unstability of Mans life, & the wretched estate the Wicked is in, at the houre of his Death; I will now also set downe, some Motives for incouragements to true Godlinesse, wherin it shall easily bee discerned, that Godlinesse excelleth Wickednesse, as farre as Light excelleth Darknesse; It is a thing, both usuall and lamentamentable, to see how men goe on in wickednesse, and can neyther bee drawne, to thinke of theyr end by the dayly examples of Mortality; nor wonne to remember, the infinitnesse of Gods Love by their dayly preservations ; they call not once to theyr remembrance, the saying of the Apostle PAVL, wherein hee admonisheth them, to worke out theyr Salvation with feare and trembling ; by which, hee depriveth them of all kind of security; and the Prophet IE-REMIAH. cryeth unto them and sayth; O earth! earth I earth I heare the Word of the Lord.

Ierem. 22.

Shew-

Shewing thereby, that howsoever they esteeme of themselves, yet, they are but dust; whose glory is but for a moment, and all theyr Pleasures, but *Deceptio visus*; For that there is no Peace (saith the Lord) of the Wicked. *Esa.* 48.

Wherefore, consider this yee that forget GOD, least he teare you in pieces, and there bee none to deliver you; feare this God, for he is iust; love this God, for hee is Mercifull; stand in awe and Sinne not, commune with your hearts, consider your wayes, make your Peace with him, seeke the Lord, whilest he may bee found; If his wrath *Psal.* 14.

Psal. 2.

wrath be kindled, yea but a little, bleſſed are all thoſe that puts theyr truſt in him.

O taſte, and ſee ! how good GOD is, he is a God of Mercies, and delights not in the Death of a Sinner, as hee ſayth; Have I any pleaſure at all, that the Wicked ſhould dye, ſayth the Lord ; and not that hee ſhould returne from his wayes and live : hee will bee found of them that ſeeke him, hee hath ingaged his word for it, and againe he ſaith ; Thoſe that come to mee, I will not caſt away ; nay, hee calleth with aboundance of love : Come unto mee, all yee that

Ezech.18.

Math.11.

that are wearie and heavie
laden with the burthen of
your sinnes, and I will ease
you; hee is that good Sa-
maritaine, he may powre
in Wine to make those
wounds of your Sinnes to
smart, but hee will againe
refresh you with the oyle
of his Mercies: O then!
prostrate thy selfe at his
at his feete, creepe under
the wing of his compassi-
on; for he is slow to wrath
and of much mercy, and repenteth him of the euill: a-
las! it was thy weakenesse
that made thee sinfull, and
thy sins haue made the miserable, & thy miserie must
now sue to his mercie; if
thy misery were without
sinne,

Ioel. 2.

sinne, then thou mightest pleade before his Iustice, and his Iustice would releeue thee; but for that it proceedeth from sinne, approach the barre of his mercy, and thou shalt finde the lustre thereof to shine through all his workes; remember Christs *Math. 15.* owne words were: I am not sent, but to the lost sheepe of the house of *Israel*; what, though with the woman in the Gospell, he call thee dogge, wilt thou therefore leaue off thy sute; consider, that the tender mother many times for faults committed by her childe, hideth her louing countenance and as it were alto-

altogether reiecteth it, not
for any hatred she beareth
to the childe, but thereby
to indere the obtaining of
his favour, and to cause the
greater feare of offending;
if then, thou seasing thy
sute goeth without mercy,
whome wilt thou accuse:
Christ sayd to *Ierusalem*,
Thy destruction is of thy
selfe, O *Ierusalem*! but in
me, is thy saluation. Christ
came not, to call the righteous, but sinners to repentance.

Hee is infinitely good,
and hurteth no man, vnlesse
the blame be in himselfe,
through his owne default;
for, as the Sunne beame, is
cleare and comfortable in
it

it felf, and fo is it to the eye
that is found, yet to a fore
eye, it is very grieuous, not
through any default in the
funne, but by the difeafed
difpofition of the eye; fo
albeit, he in himfelfe, be
perfectly good, and doth
nothing but good; yet to an
vnrepentant finner he is
grieuous and terrible, but if
he returne to him by vnfai-
ned repentance, he foone
inclineth to mercy; as is e-
uident in that woman,
whom Chrift fo called; upon her humiliation and
acknowledging her fefe
to be no better, fhe recei-
ueth this gracious anfwer;
Be it vnto thee euen as thou
wilt; and againe, in the *Ne-*
niuites;

nivites; though his decree was gone out against them, that yet forty dayes, and *Ninivie* should be destroyed, upon their unfained repentance, he also repented of that euill, and with aboundance of mercy revoked that sentence; For the eyes of the Lord, beholds all the earth, to strengthen them, that with a perfect heart beleeve, and hope in him; and againe, it is sayd, O how good is the Lord, unto them, that put theyr trust in him, and to the Soule that seeketh after him; never was there any forsaken, that put theyr trust in him: and though the hand of your Faith, be not

Ionah. 3.

: Chro.16

Lament. 3

not strong enough to lay
fast hold on him, as I A-
C O B did, who sayd; I will
not let thee goe, unlesse
thou blesse mee; yet, if hee
perceiue thee creeping after him, hee will imbrace
thee, for hee hath sayd;
The bruised Reede, I will
not breake, and the smoa-
king Flaxe, I will not
quench; that is, hee will
not reiect the desires of
the heart, though in weake
measure, if unfeyned, and
what he hath promised, is
Truth.

Hee loueth not, as man
loueth; for they in prosperity will regard vs, but if
Afflictions or wants come,
they regard us not; but
so

Gen. 32.

Math. 12.

so farre is our good God
from this, that his belo-
ved Sonne CHRIST IE-
SVS, tooke our shape up-
on him, suffering Hunger,
Cold, Nakednesse, Con-
tempt, and Scornings; for
his owne mouth testified,
That the Foxes had Holes,
and the Birds of the Ayre
had Nests, but the Sonne
of Man, had not whereon
to lay his head; showing
thereby to us, how farre
hee was from contemning
our Povertie, or refusing
us for our wants; let us
therefore, flie to this God,
who will not fayle us nor
forsake us: let us cast our
care upon him, for hee
careth for us, and let us first
seeke

seek the Kingdome of heaven and the righteousnesse thereof, and all things else shall bee ministred unto us.

How many haue beene knowne, which haue gayned to themselues, Riches, or Honours, by unlawfull meanes, that haue prospered, but if for a time they haue seemed to doe well, their Posteritie haue come to ruine, and theyr owne ill-gathered treasure, like a dilating Gangrene, hath rotted theyr owne memory, and consumed euery part of theyr heyres possession; seeming as it were, a Curse and doome, intayled with the land upon the

suc-

successour, and so proveth, not a Blessing , but the bane of him that Injoyed it.

They may for a time, flourish like a Bay Tree, but suddainely they fade and their place is no where to bee found. Oh therefore ! that they would consider, what great evils, and how many inconveniences, this small prosperity bringeth with it, they should find this love of Riches, more to afflict, by desire, then to delight, by use : for it inwrappeth the Soule, in divers temptatiós, & bindeth it in infinit cares, it allureth it with sundry delights,

C 5   pro-

provoketh it to sinne, and disturbeth the quiet, no lesse of the body then of the Soule, and that which is greater; Riches are never gotten, without troubles, nor possessed, without care, nor lost, without griefe; but that which is worst, they are seldome gathered, without sinne and offence to GOD? Why then, should man bee so greedy of this Worlds pelfe, life beeing so short, and death following at our heeles? What neede is there of so great Provision, for so short a Iourney? What would man doe with so great Riches; especially, seeing that the

lesse

leſſe he hath, the more
lightly and freely hee may
walke, and when hee ſhall
come to the end of his
Pilgrimage, if he be poore,
his eſtate ſhall not be wor-
ſer then rich mens, who
are loden with much gold;
the Grave ſhall both alike
containe them, as ſayth
Iob ; The ſmall and great *Iob. 3.*
are there, and the Servant
is free from his Maſter.

Nay, it is better with
the poore, then with the
rich ; for they ſhall ſecle
leſſe griefe in parting with
this traſh and pelfe of the
World, and a ſmaller ac-
compt is to be rendred before G o d ; whereas on
the other ſide, Rich men
     D   leaves

leaves theyr Mountaines of Gold, with great griefe of heart, which they adored as G O D; neyther are they, without exceeding gerat hazard and danger, in rendring an accompt for them: Besides, as hee came forth of his Mothers

Ecclef 5. Wombe, so naked shall he returne, to goe as hee came; and shall take nothing of his labour which he may carry away in his

Pſalm. 7. hand: Therefore a little that a Righteous man hath, is better then the Riches of many wicked. I have seene sayth DAVID, in the same Pſalme; The wicked in great power, and spreading himselfe like a greene

Bay

Bay tree, yet hee passed away, and loe hee was not; I sought him but hee could not bee found, the transgressoars shall be destroyed together, the end of the Wicked shall bee cut off; but marke the upright man, and behold the Iust, for the end of that man is Peace.

Thrice blessed then is that man, that feareth God, and they whose God the Lord is, and he that sets his feare alwayes before his eyes; For they shall bee delivered out of sixe troubles, and in the seaventh, no evils shall touch them, in Famine, he shall redeeme them from

Iob. 5.

D 2   Death,

Death, and in Warre, from the power of the sword, they shall come to the Grave in a full age, like as a shocke of Corne commeth in, in his season: They may for a time bee hungry, but they shall be filld, for God himselfe will feed them with blessings from aboue and from beneath. Even naturall reason will not suffer them to doubt, for he that giveth meate in due season, to Ants and Wormes of the Earth, will he suffer Man to famish, who night and day, serue and obey him, as CHRIST himselfe saith in MATTHEVV; Behold the Fowles of the heaven, for

Math. 6.

for they fow not, neyther reape nor cary into Barnes, yet your heavenly Father feedeth them, are yee not much better then they; This happines moved DAVID to invite us to ferve the Lord, faying; O feare the Lord yee that be his Saints, for they that feare the Lord lack nothing, the Lyons doe lacke and fuffer hunger, but they that feeke the Lord, fhall want no manner of thing that is good.

The ungodly man, when he is full of wealth dyeth for hunger, and when they fit even up to the lips in water, yet they are flaine with thirft, as the Poets

Pfalm. 34

D 3   in

in times paſt, fabled of TANTALVS. But though many and great be the troubles of the Righteous, yet the Lord delivereth them out of all. For the eyes of the Lord is over the Righteous, and his Eare is open to theyr cry, but the Face of the Lord is againſt them that do evill, to cut off theyr Remembrance from the Eatth.

Who would be unwilling then, to ſuffer ignominies and ſcornings, rather then with the wicked, to injoy the pleaſures of Sin for a ſeaſon ; God himſelfe will wipe all teares from theyr eyes, hee will give them Ioyes for theyr Sorrowes,

*Pſalm.*34

Revel. 21.

rowes, as hee sayth; Blessed are yee that now Weepe, for yee shall Rejoyce, troubles in this life, are badges of Gods Children, Whom the Lord loveth, hee chastiseth, and correcteth every Sonne that he chuseth with Patience; Therefore, possesse your Soules, and remember who it is, that sayd; You are not of the World, as I am not of the World, the world hateth you, because it hated mee first, if you were of the world, the world would love you.

Prov. 3.

Luke, 21.

John, 15.

Oh, blessed Sufferings! that makes us like to God himselfe, if wee had the Wisedome of SALOMON,

D 4   the

the Treasure of CRŒSVS, and the long life of METHVSALEM, and out of the favour and love of God, our Wisedome were Foolishnesse, for to know him, is perfect wisedome, our Riches were drosse; for riches will not avayle in the day of Wrath, and that life, so long and wickedly led, no better, then a man that dreames hee is a King, honoured of all and wanting nothing, when waking, hee findes himselfe hated of all, and wanting all things.

III.

III.

Of the Peace of a good Conscience, and the Ioyfull end of the Godly.

SALOMON, having set himselfe to behold all things that were under the Sun, & having taken to himselfe, all that could bee delightfull, for what can he dce more that commeth after the King, at last concludeth; That all the dayes of Man, are sorrowes, and his travailes, griefe; therefore sayth he; I hated life, for all is Vanity and vexation

Eccles.2.

D 5   of

of Spirit; and perceiving how apt men were, to follow what delights this world could affoord them, scoffes at theyr folly, and by way of derision sayth: Rejoyce O young man in thy Youth, & let thy heart cheare thee in the dayes of thy youth, and walke in the wayes of thine heart, and in the sight of thine eyes, yet would hee not let them goe on thus, but gives them an *Item*, saying; But know, that for all these things, God will bring thee to Iudgement, for though, sayth hee: A Sinner doe evill an hundred times, and his dayes bee prolonged; yet surely

Ecclef. 11

I

I know, that it shal be well with them, that feare God.

These Caveats, the godly man placeth before his remembrance, least hee should fall into errors, and making his life of no value to him, hee despiseth all things, onely ayming at that, may make him happy, which is, a good Conscience, for that will bring him peace at the last; death being to a godly man, the ending of Sorrowes, and the beginning of Ioyes; he doth then begin to live with God, when hee dyes to the World, as it is sayd in *Ecclesiastes* ; Who so feareth the Lord, it shall goe well with him at. the last,

Ecclesi:

last, and in the day of his Death, hee shall be blessed.

And St. IOHN, was commanded to Write: Blessed are the Dead, that dye in the Lord, even so sayth the Spirit; that they may rest from theyr labours, & their works follow them. How can that man bee discouraged, that heareth this of the Lord, in the houre of his Death; when he findeth himselfe hasting thither, where hee shall receive that, which he hath all his life-time desired.

And Saint AVGVSTINE, speaking of the Death of a Good man, sayth; He that desireth to bee dissolved, & be with *Christ*; dyeth not Patiently, but liveth Patiently,

*Revel.*14.

ently, and dyeth delight-
somely, and it may be sayd;
That like a Swan, he dyeth
singing, yeilding the glory
to God which calleth him.
With what joy, doth that
Soule behold his end, who
hath all his Life-time possessed a good Conscience,
nothing fearefull, can present it selfe before him, he
sees all his sinnes, not of a
Crimson die, but White as
wooll, washed by the blood
of Christ; he beholds him,
not as his Iudge, but his
Sauiour and Mediatour,
his Iudge is his Brother,
God in Christ is become
his Father, hee hath no
debts to pay, *Christ Iesus*
on the Crosse hath Can-
celled

celled the hand writing
that was againſt him, and
hath not onely made him
free, but alſo an heyre of
the Kingdome of Heaven.
The preſence of Death, is
not terrible to him, for
he feareth not Death, be-
cauſe hee feared G O D,
and hee that feareth him
need feare none other : hee
feareth not Death, becauſe
he feared Life, but feare of
Death, are the effects of an
evill Life ; hee feareth not
Death, becauſe through all
his life hee learned to dye,
and prepared himſelfe to
dye ; but a man prepared
and provident, need not
feare his Enemy ; he fea-
reth not Death, becauſe ſo
long

long as he lived; he fought
for thofe things that
might helpe him, that is,
for Vertues and good
Workes; hee feareth not
Death, becaufe to a Righ-
teous man, Death is not
death, but a fleepe, it is not
Death, but an end of all labours, it is not Death but
a way unto life, and a Ladder unto Paradice; for hee
knoweth, that Death hath
loft all the bitterneffe of
Dea h, after it hath paffed
through the veynes of
Life, and that it hath received the fweetneffe of life :
hee feareth not the pre-
fence of Divels, becaufe he
hath CHRIST his defen-
der and Captaine : he feareth

reth not the horror of the grave, because he knoweth that his body is sowne a corruptible body, but shall rise againe, in incorruptible body, often boasting in the strength hee hath gained by *Christ*, saying with cheerefulnesse of spirit; O Death, where is thy sting? O Grave, where is thy victory? The strong man, death comes not upon him unawares; for hee hath layd up in store for himselfe a good foundation against this time, which was to come, that hee might lay hold on Eternall life.

Even the brest-plate of righteousnesse, the shield of

2. *Cor.* **15.**

1. *Tim.* **6.**

Ephes. **5.**

of Faith, the Helmet of Salvation, and the Sword of the Spirit, having his loynes girt about with verity, and his feete shod with the preparation of the Gospell of Peace, what hope now hath his enemy of any advantage, though helped by the weakenesse of his owne flesh : Death was ever expected, and therefore provided for : he alwayes lived as in the presence of GOD, having a strict eye over all his actions, and though now Satan bend all his Forces against him, because hee hath but a small time, before his siege must bee raysed, and therefore presents

that

that before him which he
deareſt loued, his Wife,
Children, Father, and
Friends, with his whole
Eſtate, Honour, Riches,
Youth, Health, Strength,
and Life it ſelfe, thereby
thinking to ſhake his
hold ; for this ſubtill eni-
my knoweth, they are not
loſt without griefe, which
are poſſeſsed with Love;
yet fayles he of his pur-
poſe, for it is certaine, hee
that in this life knoweth
of feweſt delights, leaſt of
all other, feareth Death, ſo
he having never prized
them otherwayes then
they were in themſelves,
parteth from them with
the leſſe trouble, yet weake
nature

nature strugling with him,
may a little dazle him,
but calling to minde the
Words of his Saviour,
who sayth: He that forsa-
keth Father, Mother,
Wife, Children, house and
lands, for my sake, shall
receive an hundred fold,
hee gaines strength, and
with the greater joy his
Soule answers? Oh sweet
Iesvs! shall I not willingly forgoe all these, who
for my sake, suffered the
Viols of thy Fathers wrath
due to me for sinne, to be
powred out upon thee, and
in thy body indured that,
which I deserved? It was
for my sake, thou wast
borne in a Stable, and layd
in

Mark. 10.

in a Cratch ; for me, thou
flying into Egypt , livedst
feaven yeares in banish-
ment ; for me, thou didst
fast, thou didst watch, thou
didst run hither & thither,
thou didst sweate Water
and Bloud , thou didst
Weepe, and thou didst
prove by experience, those
miseries which my sinnes
deserved ; and yet thou
wast without sinne, ney-
ther was there guile found
in thy mouth , neyther
hadst thou offended , but
wast offended; for me, thou
wast taken, forsaken of
thine, denyed, sold , bea-
ten with fists, spet upon ,
mocked, whipped, crow-
ned with Thornes, reviled
with

with blasphemies, hanged upon the Crosse, Dead, and Buried, thou wert not onely forsaken of all externall things, but also of the Divine comfort, as thy owne Mouth testified, when thou cryedst out, *My God, my God, why hast thou forsaken mee*; Oh the height of Love! Oh the depth of unmeasurable humility! Oh the greatnesse of Mercy! Oh the bottomlesse Pit of incomprehensible Goodnes: Oh Lord! if I be so greatly indebted to thee, because thou hast redeemed mee, what doe I not owe thee, for the manner by which thou hast redeemed mee:
thou

Math. 27.

thou haſt redeemed mee with moſt great dolours; with contumelies, and ignominies, not to be borne; inſomuch, that thou waſt made a reproach of men, and the ſcorne of the whole world; through thy reproaches, thou haſt honoured me; through thy accuſations, thou haſt defended me; through thy bloud, thou haſt waſhed me; through thy death, thou haſt rayſed me; and through thy teares, thou haſt freed me, from everlaſting weeping and gnaſhing of teeth: thine were the Wounds, that healed my ſores: thine was the backe, that bare my my forrowes ; thine was the prize, that quit my fcores : thou affumedft my flefh, to redeeme me here, and thou raigneft as King, to crowne me here-after. Thus by thofe mife-rable Torments, thou didft freeme from all evill ; and fhall I be unwilling to fuf-fer the deprivation of a lit-tle happineffe, and the in-during of a few paines to come unto thee, who haft thus dearely purchafed me for thy felfe : thefe Medi-tations fo ravifhed his foule, that with Saint PAVL he thinkes himfelfe in the third Heaven, hee hath drunke fo freely of the Ri-ver of Paradice, one drop of of which is greater then the Ocean, which alone is able to quench the thirst of the whole World, that he loatheth these puddell Waters, accounting all things but drosse and dung in respect of *Christ*, all is to him in comparison, no more then the light of a Candle, is to the glorious beames of the Sunne, he is now so farre from esteeming eyther them, or life, that he desires to be dissolved and be with *Christ*, he longs for the day of his dissolution, life being to him a Prison, and with often groanes and sighes, cryeth, *Come Lord Iesu, come quickly*; and with

DA.

DAVID hee fayth: O how
I long to appeare before
GOD. If life were offe-
red him, with all the pleafures thereof, hee would
defpife it, for hee is fitted
for God, he is no man for
the World, his Soule hath
too exactly looked into
the worth of it, to be de-
ceived with all the glittering fhewes thereof, the
which hee findes to bee
vayne and fleeting, and
nothing permanent in this
Life.

E   IIII.

IIII.

*Of the deferring of Re-
pentance, how dange-
rous it is, and of the
deceiveablenesse of
worldly Pleasures.*

Aving now seen
the quiet Hap-
pinesse, and hap-
pie Blessednesse
of the Godly, at the houre
of his Death, mee thinkes
it should incourage every
man to prepare himselfe
for his end; in the time of
Prosperity, least when the
time of changing shall
come, they bee found na-
ked and bare, and so lye
open

open to all the assaults and
batteries of Sathan, many
there bee; to whom the
Day of Iudgement seemes
terrible, not remembring
the day of theyr Death,
which is the first Iudge-
ment, the which whosoe-
ver passeth, on such the second shall have no power;
as Saint IOHN sayth in the
Revelation : The defer-
ring of Repentance proves
dangerous. Yet some ir-
religious man will say;
When I am come to old
Age, I will runne to the
remedy of Repentance:
Dare mans frailtie presume
thus much of himselfe,
seeing hee hath not one
day of all his Life, in his

E 2 owne

owne power, for though God hath promised Pardon to the Penitent; yet he hath not promised to morrow to a sinner: therefore, whilst it is called to day, heare his voyce and hearden not your hearts, *Heb. 5.* least you enter into temptation. Follow the counsell of that Kingly Preacher, make no tarrying to *Ecclef. 5.* turne unto the Lord; and put not off from day to day, for sodainly shall his wrath come, and in the time of vengeance, he shall destroy thee: besides, there is another evill; sinne having no restraint, but free liberty, to runne on in his owne current; how dange-

dangerous doth it proove,
and how hard is it to stop
the courfe thereof, being
once growne to a cuftome:
Is it not ufually knowne,
that hee that driveth a
Nayle into a Poft, fafteneth
it at the firft ftroke that he
giveth it, but more firme-
ly at the fecond ftroke,
but fo faft at the third,
that it can hardly bee pulled out againe; and the
oftner he ftriketh it, the
fafter it fticketh, and is
pulled out againe, with
the greater difficulty: So
in every one of mans wic-
ked actions, vice is driuen
deepely into their foules,
as if it were with a Mallet,
and there it fticketh fo

E 3 faft,

fast, that it can by no
meanes be pulled foorth,
but by the bitter teares of
Repentance, which are
seldome and very hardly
found; this same thing
our Saviour shewed in the
raysing of LAZARVS, be-
ing foure dayes dead;
whom he called foorth,
with groaning of spirit:
whereas he raysed others
that were dead, with farre
easier tokens of difficulty;
signifying to us thereby,
how great a myracle it is,
that God should convert
one buried in the custome
of sinning; yet, not considering these things, how
doth time passe on, and
what numberlesse sinnes
are

Iob. 1.

are committed, without feare to offend, or care to provoke him to anger; through whofe Gates thou muft enter, before whofe feet thou muft lye proftrate, will thou nill thou; whofe mercy thou muft fue and deplore. Thou art plunged in the Gulfe of finne, he onely muft rayfe thee? thou art wounded, he onely can heale thee? thou art ficke to the death, hee onely can give thee life? Oh then, feare to offend him! of whofe helpe thou standeft in need every moment, tremble to provoke him to anger, who hath for unrepentant finners, prepared a deepe and

Ifa. 30.

E 4   large

large pit, the Piller thereof is fire and much wood,
the breath of the Lord,
like a streame of brimstone
doth kindle it; beware of
going on in delights, without remembring your end,
left you be like the Fifhes,
that fports themfelves fo
long in the delightfome
ftreames of the River *Jor-
dan*; that unawares they
plunge themfelves in *Ma-
re mortuum*, from whence
there is no Redemption;
many are the baytes and
fnares, which are layd for
man in this life, cove-
red over with glittering
wealth, and delightfome
Pleafures, but bare thefe
deceits, and caufe them to
appeare

appeare in their own like-
nesse, and thou shalt finde
this World to bee a Caf-
ket of forrowes and grie-
vances, a Schoole of Vanity, a laborinth of Errors,
a dungeon of Darknesse,
a Market place of Coufo-
nages, a way beset with
Theeves, a ditch full of
mud, and a Sea continual-
ly tost and troubled with
stormes and Tempests :
what other thing is the
world, but a barren Land,
a field full of Thistles
and Weeds, a Wood full
of Thornes, a flourishing
Garden, but bringing forth
no fruit, a River of Teares,
a Fountaine of Cares, a
sweet poyson; A Tragedy

E 5   plea-

pleasantly framed, a delightfull Phrenzie; the Worlds rest hath labour, the Security of it without ground, the feare of it is without cause, the Labour of it without fruit, the Teares without purpose, and the puposes without successe, the Hope of it is vayne, the joy feyned, and the Sorrow true, the Glory of this World, is but the singing of Syrens, sweet, but a deadly Potion, a Viper, artificially painted without, but within full of venemous poyson: If the World fawne upon thee, it doth it that it may deceive thee; if it Exalt thee, it doth it that thy fall may

may bee the greater; if it
make thee merry, it doth
it that it afterwards with
forrow may breake thy
heart; it giveth all her
goods with a mixture of
incomparable heavineſſe
and griefes, and that with
the greateſt uſurie: if a
Sonne bee borne to thee
and ſoone after dye, thy
forrow willbe ſeaven fold
greater then was thy Ioy,
the thing loſt, more afflic-
teth, then found joyeth;
Sickneſſe more excrucia-
teth, then Health glad-
deth; Injury more tormen-
teth, then Honour conten
teth; to conclude, what
good things are found in
the World, which are not
coun-

counterfeit, and what e-
vill which are not so in-
deed; if these things be so
indeed as they are, wherefore should man desire to
stay any longer in this land
of *Ægypt* to gather stub-
ble, who would not flye
out of this *Babilon*, who
would not desire to be delivered from this fire of
Sodome and *Gomorrah*: seeing therefore, that the
World is beset with so
many snares, and that so
many downfals and break-
neckes are in the way, and
the flame of Vices doe so
burne us, who at any time
can bee secure and safe, as
Prov. 6. the Wife man fayth; Can
a man take fire in his bo-
some

some, and his cloathes not be burnt, or can a man goe upon Coales, and his feet not burnt; he that toucheth Pitch, shallbe defiled with the same; estrange then thy minde from these ycie Vanities; listen and thou shalt heare CHRIST, who seeth the danger thou art falling into, calling unto thee, that hee may teach thee a way to prevent thy hurt, and saying; Behold, I stand at the doore and knocke, runne and open to this Physitian of thy Soule. O refuse him not, neyther delay his entrance, for thou art sicke, and he will give thee to drinke of the water of Life, neyther for

Eccles. 13.

for money, nor by mea-
sure, but freely, and taking
thy fill, without limitation,
and freely too, being of
his owne Grace and
Mercy.

Can you then, knowing
to whom you are to open,
stand with delayes; as I
cannot yet, I will anon, but
this I cannot yet, I will a-
non; is deferred so long,
that this heavenly ghest
goeth away without a
Lodging, by reason of
which, he will hardly bee
brought againe, without
many teares: Oh then bee
ready at the first knock to
open; I meane the first
good motion, so shall you
receive a ghest, whose
                    compa-

company is sweeter, then the honey and the honey Combe: Oh heart! more hard then stone, that can refuse him; if considered who it is, it is CHRIST, the well-beloved Sonne of his Father, it is hee, in whom, God the Father is so well pleased, that all thy sinnes are forgiven, being covered with the robe of his Righteousnesse; it is he, that suffered Rebukes, Buffetings, Scornings, Spittings on, and at the last, death; I, and that, the most cursedst death, even the death of the Crosse, as it is written: Cursed are every one that hang on a Tree.

Galat. 3.

These things being so, have.

have you not hearts harder then an Adamant, thus to oppose his entrance : Oh doe not deferre this purchase to the time to come, for one minute of this time (which now vainely flydeth from thee) is more precious, then the Treasure of the whole world.

Math. 13. Be like unto a wise Marchant, that having found a precious Pearle, goes and sels all he hath to purchase it; what thing more precious then the Sonne of God, which heere offereth himselfe unto thee ? why art thou so slacke in giving him entertainement, thinkest thou him not worthy, because thou beholdest him

him in his Humility, poore
and despised, or doth thy
flesh puffe thee up with a
conceit beyond thy me-
rites, if it doe, cast thy
eyes upon thy selfe, and
consider what thou wast
before thou wast borne,
what thou art now, being
borne, and what thou shalt
bee after Death : before
thou wast borne, thou wast
filthy and obsceane mat-
ter, not worthy to be na-
med ; now thou art dung,
covered over with snow,
and a while after thou
shalt be meat for Wormes:
why then, shouldest thou
bee proud, seeing thy Na-
tivity is sinne, thy Life misery, and thy End putrifac-
tion

tion and corruption.

Having confidered thus
with thy felfe, tell mee if
thou haft not the greater
reafon to open with the
more celerity, hee of himfelfe, being willing to
paffe by thefe thy Infir-
mities, wouldeft thou
not account that man moft
heatheni∫h, who having a
Friend, that had indured
feaven yeares imprifon-
ment, to keepe him from
that bondage, & at the laft
payed his Ranfome, at fo
deare a rate, as thereby his
eftate were for ever rui-
ned, otherwife hee him-
felfe to indure perpetuall
Slavery : if this man, I fay,
fhould come and knocke
at

Semel.

at the doore of his Friend,
desiring admittance, and
acquainting him, with
who it was, and hee for
this his love, should seeme
not to know him, but bid
him be gone and barre the
doore against him; I know
thou wouldest account
him most inhumane and
ungratefull, and yet how
farre short comes this of
CHRIST's love and boun-
ty to thee, for the cha-
stisement of thy Peace,
was layd upon him, and
with his stripes thou wast
healed.

Isa. 53.

O wretched Soule ! to
loose such a Friend, Oh un-
happie man ! by this op-
position, to deprive thy
selfe

selfe of all Happines : for
what greater Happinesse
canst thou have, then to
injoy that Fatherly provi-
dence by which God pre-
serveth his, what swee-
ter Delights, then the Divine Grace, the Light of
wisedome, the consolations
of the holy Ghost, the Ioy
and Peace of a good Con-
science, the good event of
Hope, the true liberty of
the Soule, the inward
peace of the Heart, to bee
heard in Prayer, to be helped in Tribulations, to be
provided for temporall ne-
cessities, and to bee ayded
and to taste of Heaven-
ly Comforts in death :
whilst I seriously me-
ditate

ditate upon these things,
my Soule is as in a Rapture,
me thinkes I see CHRIST
IESVS comming in the
Clouds, with thousand of
Angels about him, the
Heavens and Earth flying
away at his presence, mil-
lions of damned Soules,
yelling and crying to the
Rocks and Mountaines, to
fall upon them, and to cover them, from the fierce-
nesse of his sight; The Divels quaking and trembling
expecting the denouncing
of their Torments; and
the Ioyes the Godly have
at that houre: For as it is a
day of horror and terror to
the Wicked, so is it a day
of joy and gladnesse to the
godly;

godly ; for as the body of the one rests in the earth, without taste of those miseries it hath deserved; even so the Righteous, by this sleepe of Death, is deprived of this blessednesse in their body, untill corruption hath put on incorruption, and mortality hath put on immortality ; and that they are wakened by the sound of the Trumpet;which simoneth them to appeare before CHRIST; when then their soules become againe reunited to their bodyes, and both with Ioy,beholds the face of God , not as their Iudge, for he is their Brother ; and therefore

can

can expect from him, no-
thing but mercy; he hath
purchased them for him/
felfe, with no meaner a
a price, then, his owne
precious bloud; and therefore, must needs bee to him
acceptable, this is theyr
yeare of *Iubilee*, this is the
Marriage of the Lambe,
with him they enter, and
he is theyr God, and they
are his Sonnes; they now
behold his face, and his
Name is in theyr fore-
heads; They now, receive
the fulnesse of theyr Ioy,
they now, possesse that happinesse theyr Soules thir-
sted for; they now, injoy
the reward of all theyr labours; this blessednesse
truly

Revel.21.

Revel.22.

truly confidered on, af-
foordeth more pleasures
then the tongue of Man
can utter, or his Soule remayning in the Prifon of
his flefh, is able to receive,
without crying out with
the Spoufe in the *Canticles*:
I am ficke of Love. It is
no marvell, that the Church
cryeth ; Come Lord I s-
s v s, come quickly: for
in this his comming, con-
fifteth all happineffe. Here
is the finall end of all miferies and finnes ; it onely,
prooveth the waters of
Mara to the ungodly ; it is
terrible to none, but the
unrepentant, even they
who had their eyes fealed
from beholding any other
happi-

Cant. 2§

Happines, then what tended to their pleasures; They which tooke to them the Timbrell and the Harp, and rejoyced in the sound of the Organs, they spend theyr dayes in wealth, and were of them that sayd: Speake no more to us in the name of the Lord, they sayd to God, depart from us, for wee desire not the knowledge of thy wayes. What is the Almighty, that we should serve him? and what profit shall wee have, if we pray unto him? Now alas! but too late, they see theyr owne follyes; now without hope of redresse, they behold theyr owne miseries; no marvell,

F though

though the mentioning of the day of Iudgement, be terrible to such a man; who by his wickednesse, deprives himselfe of all those Blessednesses; for ill will it prove, if the day of Death, be not alwayes in his remembrance; which is the first judgement, and wherein he must stand eyther convicted, or acquitted; eyther condemned for his bad workes, or justified for his good, whereof he can have little hope, unlesse hee meet his Iudge in the way, and make his peace with him, whilst he may be found; yet, there is time to furnish thy lamp with Oyle, yet the Gates of

of Mercy are not shut, yet
thou mayest so cry, as
thou mayest bee satisfied
with this gracious answer;
Come yee blessed of my Fa-
ther; Whereas, if thou deferre thy Repentance from
time to time, putting farre
from thee the evill day, if
thou doe not expect the
comming of thy Lord, but
become drunken, and fall
to smiting thy fellow Servants, if thou hide thy Ta-
lent in the Earth, which
God in his goodnesse hath
bestowed on thee to better
uses: Thy Lord will come
when he is not looked for,
and in a time when thou
art not aware of, and cast
thee into utter Darknesse,

Math. 21.

F 2 where

where fhall bee wayling
and gnafhing of Teeth, giving thee a juft hyre for
thy careleffe fecurity : It is
not thy pleafures, that can
deferre thy calamities; it is
not the inlarging thy
Barnes, that can refift thy
mifery ; the greatneffe of
Friends will not availe; thy
Iudge is blinde to Bribery,
and deafe to all but Iuftice,
if his wrath be not appeafed before he come to give
fentence, it will then be
too late to expect mercy.

V.

V.

Comforts for the weake Christian ; and to beware of Backesliding.

OVR most subtile malicious Enemy retayning still the hatred hee bare our first Parents at the beginning, seeketh to bring us into everlasting Perdition, and so to gaine us to himselfe by one meanes or other; to a man nouzeled in Sinne, hee useth no other wayes, then the lulling him still the faster

F 3   asleepe

asleepe in worldly plea-
sures; the Miser he perswa-
deth still to covet Riches,
thereby making his Gold
his God; by which meanes
hee filleth up the measure
of Wrath against the day
of Iudgement: the Adulte-
rer hee draweth on more
easily, by the delightsom-
nesse of the sinne, telling
him that stolne bread is
sweet, and hid waters
pleasant: the Proud man,
hee hath hud-wincked,
not to thinke of time, but
to account all lost, but what
is spent in decking and
setting himselfe foorth in
the Divels Feathers: Thus
all sinnes he lessens, that so
he may cause man to defer
his

Prov. 9.

his repentance till the laſt,
then the which, there is
nothing more dangerous :
but when he meets a child
in religion, who is glad to
ſuck milke from the ſweet
paps of Gods word, him he
ſo toſſeth & ſhaketh, with
telling him of his owne
unworthines, and the ſeve-
rity of Gods Iuſtice, that
the poore Soule is ready
to leave his hold and to fall
into deſperation , not da-
ring ſcarce to looke up to
Gods Mercy ; but if his
weaknes become ſtrength
and he be rayſed by Faith,
then hee ſtrives to cauſe
him to become weary and
backward in well doing,

Therefore, thou O man !
F 4   that

that wouldest doe the good thou doest not, but through the deceiveable-nesse of thy flesh standeth loytering, and with SA-LOMONS sluggard cryeth; Yet a little sleepe, a little slumber; awake and behold CHRIST comming in the Clouds. Stand up and gird thy selfe like a man, lift up thy eye of Faith and behold thy Saviour, whose merits plead for thee? See him dying for thee, and thereby paying thy debts? See thy Iudge a just one, and therefore will not require that againe, which Christ hath already satisfied, hee hath beheld the thoughts of thine heart, and found thy

desires,

desires, are to serve him concerning the inward Man, and though thou didst fall into sinnes most offensive to the eyes of his Divine Maiesty, yet hee knowes, that the evill thou didst hate, that thou didst: But it was a Law in thy Members that ledde thee captive to the Law of sin: then if as a Captive forc't, it was no longer thou, but sinne that dwelled in thee. *Rom.* 7.

Let the remembrances of these Mercies, waken thy Soule from the drowsinesse of Sinne, and remember who hath sayd: Awake, thou that sleepest and arise from the Dead, and CHRIST shall give thee *Ephef.5.*

F 5

thee light ? Hee calleth thee ? Hee biddeth thee awake, let not thefe fweet calles, ftrike thee dead, as his prefence did the Keepers, who became aftonifhed, and were as dead men ; but rather let that voyce bee of as great power to thee, as it was to LAZARVS; not onely to rayfe thee from the fleepe, but alfo from the death of Sin. And bee as ready to entertaine this love as THOMAS was, who no fooner touched his Saviour, but cryed out : My Lord, and my God : Neyther deceive thy felfe, with a foothing conceit of what is not in thee ; For, the Tree is knowne

Math. 20.

Iohn. 11.

Ioh. 20.

Math. 7.

knowne by the fruit; for
men cannot gather Grapes
of Thornes, nor Figs of
Thistles: A good man, out
of the good Treasure of
his Heart, bringeth forth
good things, and an evill
man, out of the evill Treasure of his heart, bringeth
forth evill things; so that
howsoever thou mayst
seeme to the World, yet as
a shadow doth alwayes
follow the body, so feare
and desperation will at
all times, and in all places,
wayte upon an evill Con-
science.

Let not thy Faith be as
a House built upon the
Sands, which will shake
with every blast of Tempt-
                    tations,

Math. 7.

tations, or Afflictions, but found it upon the Rocke CHRIST IESVS; against which, whatsoever beateth shall returne with a greater repulse to it selfe, as not being able to move it; and having once attayned this perfection, take heed of recoyling, for CHRIST sayth, He that layeth hand upon the Plough and looketh backe, is not meet for the Kingdome of Heaven.

Luke.9.

What though the way to Heaven be narrow, and full of Difficulties? Wilt thou not therefore, beeing entred, perseuere? Who would wish or desire to walke in a way strowed

strowed with Roses, and
planted with divers fra-
grant Flowers, if the
assured end of it be death;
and who would refuse a
rough and difficult path,
that leadeth unto life; is it
not commonly seene, that
many men to attaine to
Preferment, run into most
apparent dangers, and
hazard the losse of theyr
life; (nay I know thou
wouldest doe it thy selfe)
and shall it bee trouble-
some and grievous to thee,
to doe that for thy Soule,
which thou refuseth not
to doe for thy Body ? Shall
it seeme a great thing unto thee, to suffer a little
trouble heere, that here-
after

after thou mayſt eſcape eternall torment? VVhat would not the rich covetous man buryed in Hell, willingly doe, if he might have licence to come into the World againe, that he might amend his errors? Is it meet that thou ſhouldeſt doe leſſe now, then he would doe; ſeeing, that if thou doſt perſever in thy wickedneſſe, the ſame torments remaine for thee.

He that runneth a Race leaveth not till hee come to the Gole; So run as you may obtaine: Remember Lots Wife, who looking backe became a Piller of Salt; ſo take heed, leſt thou by looking backe upon the

vani-

vanities of this life, forget
the care of thy Soule, commanded thee by God; & so
of his child, become not a
Piller of Salt, but a child
of Perdition; a man ha-
ving much riches, is still
covetous of more, and
what wealth to be compa-
red to the Soule? A thing
so great in it selfe; that
what gayneth hee, that
getteth the whole world,
and looseth his Soule;
even as great a purchase,
as hee, who having with
much Labour and great
charge, obtayned a preci-
ous Iewell, straight giueth
it for a trifle.

Nay, were it so, it were
the lesse, for that were but
the

the undoing of the body, this the loffe of the Soule; that friends againe may rayfe, this is a loffe irrecoverable : Wherefore, thinke no paynes wearifome, no labours irkfome, nor any troubles grievous, to attaine true happineffe;

2. *Cor.*4. For our light afflictions, which is but for a moment, worketh for us a farre more exceeding & eternall weight of Glory, while we looke not at the things which are feene, but at the things which are not feene ; for the things which are feene, are Temporall, but the things which are not feene, are Eternall : wherefore fetting

ting all hinderances apart, with cheerefulnesse of spirit, take up the Crosse of CHRIST, and incourage thy feeble spirit, with the saying of the Apostle PAVL : The troubles of this Life ; are not comparable to the joyes that shall bee heereafter : having therefore these promises, cleanse your selues from all filthinesse of the flesh and spirit, perfecting Holinesse in the feare of GOD.

2. *Cor.* 6.

VI.

VI.

*That Man ought to bee
wonne to follow Godli-
nesse, in respect of the
Eternall Happinesse.*

Deut. 30. Aving now set
before thee, Life
and good, Death
and evill: I de-
sire thee, to choose Life,
that both thou and thy
seed mayest live, for having
beheld, the deceiveablenes
of worldly pleasures, and
how this momentany feli-
city is attended on, by sorrow and her Confederates,
me thinks thou shouldest
be

be weary of this house of
Clay, scituated in a Wil-
dernes of miseries, which
hourly produceth Mon-
sters, that ravenously seeketh to prey on thy de-
struction: and withdraw-
ing thy mind from these
fleeting delights, elevate
thy thoughts to Heaven,
and contemplate with thy
selfe, of those Cœlestiall
pleasures; note the beauty
of the place, the glorious-
nesse of the company, and
the durablenesse of that
Happinesse, which is E-
ternity; for the beautie
of this place, this Heaven-
ly *Ierusalem*, looke into   *Reuel.21.*
the *Revelation*, and thou
shalt finde; It hath the
glory

glory of GOD, the light thereof to be like a Iasper stone, cleere as Chryftall; glorious muft it needs bee, when the Wall is of Iasper, and the City of pure gold, cleare like glaffe, and the Foundations of the Wall garnifhed with all manner of precious ftones; the twelve Gates were twelve Pearles; every feverall gate, was of one pearle; for the company, *Revel.* 15 there are Angels, and Martyrs, with the foure and twenty Elders, that offer up golden Vials full of odours, which are the Prayers of Saints; but, which is chiefe of all delights, there will be GOD himfelfe,

himselfe who will bee a
Looking-Glasse to the
eyes of his Elect, Musicke
to theyr eares, Nectar and
Ambrosia to their Palates,
odoriferous Balsamum to
theyr Smelling; There
thou shalt see, the variety
and beauty of the seasons,
the pleasantnesse of the
Spring, the brightnesse of
Summer, the fruitfulnesse
of Autumne, and the qui-
et of Winter, and there
shall bee whatsoever may
delight thy sences, and e-
very faculty of thy Soule;
there will be, the fulnesse of
light to thy understanding,
the aboundance of Peace
to thy will, and the conti-
tinuance of Eternity to
thy

thy memory ; there, the Wiſedome of SALOMON, ſhall ſeeme ignorance ; there, the beauty of AB- SASOM ſhall ſeeme defor- mity ; there, the ſtrength of SAMPSON, ſhall ſeeme weakeneſſe ; there, the long life of METHV- SALEM, ſhall ſeeme a ſpan ; there, the Riches of CRŒSVS, ſhall ſeeme droſſe : for there, thou mayſt worthily call the treaſures of all Emperors and Kings, ſtarke poverty and beggery.

These things beeing thus ? Why ſhouldeſt thou O man ! delight to begge, and live of Almes, when thou ſhalt finde ſuch a- boundance

boundance in Heaven,
looke upon thy selfe and
consider, how the Lord
hath bestowed upon thee
a countenance of Majesty,
with thy face erected to-
wards Heaven, and thy
eye-lids to move upwards,
thereby to teach thee, that
thou wert not formed, to
spend thy dayes in the moi-
ling cares of this troublesome world, but to aspire
to that true Happines, that
maketh all the other Misery.

Marke the Sea-mans
Needle, whose nature of
that Iron is, that in what
part it hath touched the
Loadstone, that part al-
wayes looketh towards
the

the North, and remaineth
unsetled, till it hath found
the Pole: even so hath God
created Man, and hath infu-
sed into him a naturall in-
clination and readinesse,
that hee should alwayes
looke to his Maker; as to
the Pole and onely true
happines.

When the Children of
Israel in the Wildernesse,
were stung by fiery Ser-
pents, none could live,
but those, that looked up
to that brazen Serpent,
which MOSES erected; so
no man beeing stung by
those fiery Serpents of sin,
can live; but those, that by
the eye of Faith looke
up to CHRIST IESVS,
behol-

beholding him, dying upon
the Croſſe, and applying
his death and merits, to
their otherwiſe deadly-
wounded Soule, whereby
that Vlcer is cured and they
aſſured of life.

After ADAM had ſin-
ned in eating the forbid-
den fruit, GOD ſent him
to Till the Earth, out of
which he was taken; but
the ſoule of man was in-
fuſed into him by the
breath of God; let there-
fore the cogitations of
thy heart and Soule bee
turned towards him, from
whence it had the beeing,
ſeeing, as ſayth Saint
AVGVSTINE: There is
nothing more bleſſed, than
this

Gen. 3.

Gen. 2.

G

this life, where there is
no feare of Poverty, no in-
firmity of Sicknesse, no
deceipts of the Divell, neyther Death of body or
Soule, but a pleasant life
through the guift of Im-
mortality, then there shall
be no mischiefes, no dif-
cords, but all agreement;
because there shall be one
concord of all the Saints,
peace and joy imbrace all
things.

What is it, that thou
canst desire heere upon
Earth, that thou shalt not
there freely possesse? If
thou desirest pleasures, lift
up thy heart and see how
delightfull that Good is,
that contayneth in it, the
delight

delight and pleasure of all good things? If this life created doth please thee, how much more shall that life please thee, which hath created all things? If health given make thee merry, how much more shall he make thee merry, that giveth all health? If the knowledge of the Creatures bee sweet, how much more sweeter shall the Creator himselfe be? If beauty bee acceptable unto thee, it is he, at whose beauty, the Sunne and Moone admire; the glory of which, was so great, that when MOSES went up to the Mount, though he saw but the hinder part

G 2   there-

thereof, his Face became so bright and shining, that the Israelites could not behold him ; what should I stand longer to set forth the beauty of that, which if I had the tongue of Men and Angels, I could not doe ; for as the Apostle sayth ; Eye hath not seene, Eare hath not heard, neyther hath it entred into the heart of Man, the things which God hath prepared for them that love him.

1. *Cor.* 2.

Wilt thou then choose with the Prodigall Sonne, to eate Huskes with the Swine, rather than to returne home to thy Heavenly Father, will not all these

these delights move thee,
nor cause thee to desire it ;
it may bee thou art timc-
rous, knowing thy owne
unworthinesse ; but bee incouraged by the words of
thy Saviour , who seeing
thy faint heartednesse,
sayth : Feare not little
flocke, for it is your fathers
pleasure to give you a
Kingdome. Thou art one
of the flocke , and this
Kingdome is prepared for
thee ; why dost thou not
long to take possession of
thy owne, purchased for
thee by CHRIST, who
though hee be thy Elder
brother ; yet thou shalt
bee co-heyre with him,
whose love , thou mayst

Luke.15.

G 3   see

see expressed, by his infinite care; for in his Prayer to his Father for his Disciples, he remembred thee, when he sayd, I pray not for these alone, but for those that shall beleeve on me, that they may all be one as thou Father art in me, and I in thee, and the glory which thou hast given mee, I have given them, that they may bee one even as wee are one, I will also, that those thou hast given mee, bee with me.

John.17.

Canst thou now have any doubts or waverings in thy Mind ? Repayre unto him, and in true humility of Soule confesse thy

thy felfe unto him , and
fay ; Father I have finned
againft Heaven and againft
thee , and I am no more
worthy to bee called thy
Sonne : This done, doubt
not but hee will imbrace
thee in the Armes of his
Mercy, the Ring and Robe
fhall be brought, and the
fatted Calfe fhall be kild :
for there is more joy in
Heaven , over one finner
that repenteth , than of
ninety and nine juft per-
fons : It is a place prepared for thee , before the
Foundation of the World
were layd. O happy Soule!
that art made poffeffor of
this bleffednelfe ! How art
thou able to behold any

thing

thing in this life, with true
contentment, having se-
rioufly beheld this; though
thou didſt dayly ſuffer
torments, if for a long
time thou didſt indure
Hell it ſelfe, ſo that at the
length thou mightest ſee
CHRIST in his glory, and
injoy this bleſſedneſſe,
and haue ſociety with
the Saints; were it not worthy all Sufferings? All
Bitternes? and all Croſſes,
that thou mightest be par-
taker of all this good. At
laſt, what though the
world account not of
thee, but deride thee for
thy vertuous living? Re-
member ELIZEVS the
Prophet of the Lord, who
was

was mocked and called *Bald-head*, in contempt; Resolve with thy selfe, no sooner to enter into the path of Godlinesse, but such is the malitiousnesse of thy Mortall Enemie, that hee will set his members in the way against thee; that if it bee possible, they may hinder thy proceedings, and turne thee backe againe into the broad way of Errors, that leadeth to destruction.

No sooner did SAVL Prophesie, but the wicked and the men of BELIAL, had him in derision, who better affected, then PAVL the Apostle, whilst he remayned a Persecutor of

G 5   CHRIST

CHRIST in his members, and carried with him the authority of the High Priests, to strengthen his proceedings; but no sooner was he converted, but how many enimies had he, which streight sought his destruction, hayling him to Prisons, to Scourging, and to Stonings to death. Yet so farre were they from being disheartned by this, as that they reioyced that they were counted worthy to suffer for the name of CHRIST.

When we enter into Baptisme, we professe to become CHRISTS souldiers, and to fight vnder his banner; and is it the part of a

Souldier

Souldier, to flye at the first
onset, he that indureth to
the end, gaineth not onely
the honour, but the reward;
nay, the fiercer the assault
is, the more we ought
to oppose our selues
against it, and though
through the roughnes of
the incounter, we may
thinke we haue the worst,
yet if with patience wee
striue to perseuer, our Captaine CHRIST IESVS will
be at hand to helpe vs, for
carefull is he of his owne,
as his owne mouth testifi-
eth; when he saith, to his
Father, All thou hast
giuen me, I haue kept, and
none of them is lost. Let
all these proofes arme thy
                        minde

minde, to be resolute in going on in goodnes, till thou
attaine the end where thou
shalt gaine the reward of
thy abours, and take with
theel, the Counsell of the
Philosopher HERMES,
who sayth, It is better, to
suffer shame for vertuous
dealing, then to win ho-
nour by vicious living.

When SALOMON had
builded the Temple and
sanctified it, none might
enter into *Sanctum Sanctorum*, the holiest of all,
but the Priest onely. So
none can enter into this
Kingdome, which is the
true *Sanctum Sanctorum*;
but those who haue by a
Religious course of life,
put

put off the vanities of this
world, and cloathed them-
selves with the Robe of
CHRISTS Righteousnesse,
whereby they are Confe-
crated & made fit to enter.

When the Children of
* Israell* were in the Wil-
dernes, they were com-
manded every day to ga-
ther Manna, but on the
Sabboth they that went to
gather, found non, for
that they were on the E-
ven to provide for that
day: so fayle not thou e-
uery day of thy life, to gather this Manna, the food
of thy soule, and to lay vp
in store against this day of
thy rest, least when thou
hopest to find, thou become
frustrate

fruſtrate, and ſo thy ſoule
ſtarue with want thereof,
feede not thy ſelfe with
hopes of entertainement,
vnleſſe thou haue furni-
ſhed thy ſelfe with the
wedding garment, neither
thinke to paſſe with one
that is counterfeit, though
neuer ſo neare the colour;
for if it be not found the
right one, thou ſhalt be taken and bound hand
and foot, and caſt into
utter darkeneſſe; therefore
it is that the Apoſtle ſayth,
Exa nine your ſelues whi-
ther yee be in the Faith,
prove your ſelue.

There are many, nay moſt
that vnderſtanding the
infinitneſſe of the happines

2. Cor. 13.

nes of this place, that with BALAAM will desire to dye the death of the Righteous, but they will not liue the life of the Righteous: because they exempt themselues from many things, in the which the wicked place theyr whole felicity, they accounting this world theyr Heauen, shall therefore finde none other hereafter, as in the parable, *Abraham* sayd to the rich man in Hell; Son remember that thou in thy life-time, received thy good things ; they were his, because in them consisted all his happines:therefore possessing of them here, he could not expect

Numb. 33

a

a future: For as the Apo-
stle saith, Be not deceiued,
God is not mocked, for
what a man soweth, that
shall he reape; for he that
soweth to the flesh, shall
of the flesh reape corruption: but he that soweth to
the spirit, shall of the spirit, reape life euerlasting.
For true blessednes, consi-
steth not in meat or drink,
or in richnesse of apparell,
but in Righteousnes and
Peace, and Ioy in the Holy
Ghost.

A man who hath beene
long kept from his father
and mother, wife or chil-
dren, by imprisonment, being once at liberty, and entred on his iourney toward
them

thē, regardeth not neither
the length of the way, the
wearisomnes of his owne
steps, nor the dangerousnes
of the places he is to passe,
but goeth on with cheare-
fulnesse and longings, till
he attaine the end, and as
a spurre to whet on his
speed, placeth before the
eye of his remembrance
the sweete content hee
shall finde at meeting, can
these earthly delights
cause a man to vndergoe so
many difficulties, and shall
not the delights which
God hath prepared for his
and whereof I haue giuen
thee a glimpse, cause thee
with much more feruen-
cie, to long to attaine to
this

this place of happinesse,
and setting a part all hinderances whatsoever, fix
thy eye of Faith vpon
those vnspeakeable plea-
sures which thy soule shall
then gayne, & in Ioy when
thou shalt meete with God
thy Fathor, Christ Iesus
thy Brother and Sauiour,
who hath by the infinite-
nes of his loue espoused
thee vnto himselfe ; and
made the possessor of Heauen, where thou shalt as
sayth Saint Avgvst. im-
brace a certaine imbracing
aboue all imbracings.

Thou shalt find a sweet-
nes aboue all sweetnesse,
thou shalt see a light aboue
all lights, thou shalt smel
a savor

a fauour aboue all fauours,
moft delectable, thou fhalt
heare a voyce aboue all
voyces for rarenes, for that
voyce doth found where
no ayre doth moue it, this
light doth fhine, where no
place doth receiue it,
this fauour doth fmell
where no blaft doth carry
it, and this imbrace is there
touched, where it is not
fundred ; to conclude if
thou defireft to inioy all
bleffedneffe, and to efcape
all kinde of punifhments,
tribulations, and miferies,
there thou fhalt find liber-
tie & freedome from them
all. The God of our Lord
I E S V S C H R I S T, the
Father of Glory, giue vn-
to

to v·, the spirit of wisdome
& knowledge of him, that
the eyes of our vnderstanding being inlightned, we
may know, what is the
hope of his calling, and
what the Riches of
the Glory of the
inheritance of
his Saints,
Amen.

O F

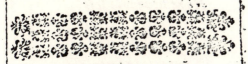

Of our losse by ADAM, and our gayne by CHRIST; The first *A-dam* was made a living Soule; the second *Adam* a quickning Spirit; For as in ADAM wee all dye, so in CHRIST, shall all be made alive. *1. Corinth. 15.*

GOD by his *Wisedame*,
  and all-seeing Pow'r
  Ordained Man
   vnto Eternitie,
Sathan through malice,
  turnes that sweet to sowre,
Man eating the forbidden Fruit
 must Die :

      No

No remedy was left
    to scape this Curse,
The sore still looked on
    became the worse.

He out of that delightsome
    place is throwne
To travell in the Warld
    with woe distresse,
Through all his life
    a Pilgrim he is knowne,
With Cares and Sorrowes,
    and with griefes oppresse:
The more he lookes
    into his wretched state,
The more he rues his fact
    but all too late.

Where-

Whereas he was
    created King of all
The Creatures
    God on Earth created had,
His Glory based is
    by this his Fall,
No creature now on Earth
    remaines so bad :
The senceleße Beaſt
    the sense of this hath found,
And having Man poßeſt
    with death doth wound.

The Earth diſdaines
    to yeeld to him her ſtrength
But pricking Thornes
    and Brambles forth doth ſend,
Till with his ſweat
    and labours ſhe at length
                 Onely

Onely for sustenance
    some food doth lend:
Thus he that was
    a heauenly Creature form'd,
By disobedience
    to a wretch is turn'd.

Of all the Trees
    that in the Garden grew,
He onely was forbidden
    that alone,
His Wife from that obedience
    soone him drew,
And taste thereof
    he did although but one:
O wretched man!
    what hast thou lost hereby
Wicked woman
    to cause thy husband dye.

'Tis

T'is not saying,
　　the Serpent thee deceiu'd,
That can excuse the fault
　　thou didst commit ;
For of all Ioyes
　　thou hast thy selfe bereau'd,
And by thy Conscience
　　thou dost stand convict.
Thy husband not alone
　　the fault must rue,
A punishment for sinne
　　to thee is due.

For as thou now conceiues
　　thy seed in sinne,
So in great sorrow
　　thou must bring it foorth,
The gaine which thou
　　by that same fruit didst winne,

Thou

Thou now doſt find
　　to bee but little worth:
Obedience to thy Husband
　　yeeld thou muſt,
And both muſt Dye
　　and turned be to Duſt.

The Truth ſometimes
　　is vſed by the Divell
When as he ſayd,
　Your eyes, ſhould opened bee,
And that you ſhould
　　diſcerne the good from euill,
When you the Fruit had taſted
　　of that tree :
But hee told not
　　your actions, ſhould be ſinne,
And Death ſhould be the good
　　which you ſhould winn.

　　　　　　　　For

For now your strength
    to weakenesse turned is,
You know the Good
    but have no powre to chuse't,
Your eyes is ope, to see
    your owne amisse,
And to behold the blisse
    you have refus'd:
You see your nakednesse
    made vilde by Sinne,
And now seekes for a place
    to hide you in.

But O alas !
    your deeds discover'd are,
You naked lye
    to those all-seeing eyes,
He viewes your actions
    and doth see you bare,

H 2   *Bare*

Bare of all Goodneſſe,
    vilde deformities:
And in your ſelves
    you have no power to mend,
For all your ſtrength, is ſinne
    Sathan doth lend.

Now ſeizes on your ſickneſſe
    Griefes and Feares,
Which night and day
    with trouble will torment ;
Your ſweet Delights,
    are turned all to teares,
And now what you haue done,
    with woe repent !
Nothing but Griefes and Feares
    and ſad annoyes,
You now poſſeſſe,
    in ſtead of endleſſe Ioyes.

                      You

You were immortall,
    but are mortall made;
You were created pure,
    but now are vilde;
Your splendant Glories
    turned all to shade;
Your Innocence
    the Devill hath beguilde:
You were created
    Children of the Lord,
But now are loathsome Dung,
    to be abhorr'd.

Which way, can you
    recouer this your losse?
What friend have you,
    that will this great debt pay?
Can you gaine, pure gold
    from filthy drosse?

H 3   Or

Or haue you power
to call againe that Day;
No, you are in
a laborinth of woe,
And endlesse is the maze
in which you goe.

Yet courage Woman,
whose weake spirit's dead,
GOD in his love
a helpe for thee hath found,
Bee sure thy Seed
shall bruise the Serpents head,
CHRIST by his Death
shall Sathan deadly wound :
This Lyon of Iudea
resist who can,
In him is blest
the whole Off-spring of man.
　　　　　　　　This

This Promise in due time
    fulfill'd hath GOD,
Vnto the comfort
    of each mortall weight;
CHRIST payes our Debt
    hee's beaten with that rod
That doth belong
    vnto our Soules of right:
His Fathers wrath
    was powred vpon him,
Which doth belong
    as due to vs for Sinne.

Hee dy'd vpon the Crosse
    and conquered Death.
That though wee dye
    yet liue againe wee must,
He buried was
    and risen is from Earth,

And raignes with God
       in Heauen amongst the Iust:
With him, our Soules and Bodies
       rais'd hath hee,
And from deaths thraldome
       now, hath set vs free:

This causeth Sathan
       stir himselfe amaine,
To see, if he can winne
       what he hath lost:
He striues to make
       our overthrow his gaine.
He stormeth now,
       that he, by CHRIST *is crost:*
And to his ayde,
       he all his forces drawes,
That he may cause vs
       to obey his Lawes.

                           Whole

Whole Armies of his Furies
　　forth he sends,
In shape transformed,
　　to delude our mindes;
And vnto them
　　his greatest force he lends,
To seize, where fittest
　　for his turne he findes:
He marks, to what men
　　are by nature given,
And vnto that,
　　he turnes his Compasse euen.

Sathan's deceipts
　　are covered, all with smiles.
That sinne seemes pleasing,
　　which our Soules destroyes,
With quaint allurements,
　　hee man still beguiles.

H 5　　　　*With*

With sweet delights
    he breeds Mans sad annoyes,
He imitates a Poyson
    rarely framed,
But once being taken
    all the life blood's stained.

Old and craftie
    is our Enemy growne,
He knowes all Fish
    at one baite will not bite,
Hee'l try a thousand wayes
    to gaine his owne,
He will not leave
    till he the marke hits right.
Some with Drunkennesse,
    Murders, Lust beside,
Others with Idlenesse,
    exessive Pride.

                   Bac-

BACCHVS *that drunken God*
   from Hell comes forth,
And reeling here and there
   few scapes his knockes,
Who shunnes his blowes
   esteem'd are of no worth,
One Drunkard at anothers
   weakenesse mockes :
What ISAIAH *saith,*
   thereon they never thinke;
Woe bee to them !
   are strong to pw'r in drinke.

GOD, *in his love*
   form'd all things for mans vse,
That for his Comfort
   they might daily be,
But they prove poyson
   through mans vilde abuse,
            Sinne

Sinne changeth all
   into deformity:
PAVL *for mans health,*
   to drinke Wine doth advise.
But through excesse,
   both Soule and Body dyes.

Man, by this Sinne
   more vile is, than a Beaſt;
For but ſufficient,
   they will never take,
Mans ſences fayles him
   ſinnes are ſtill increaſt;
He tracing vices,
   doth all good forſake:
In Drunkenneſſe,
   LOT *doth to Inceſt fall,*
NOAH *in his Wine,*
   his ſecrets ſhewes to all
                              Then

Then Lust, and Murther
   hands together take,
Like full fed Beasts,
   they neigh at neighbours wife,
Stolne bread is sweet,
   hid water theyr thirsts slake,
They fall to Murther,
   through discord and strife.
For when mans reason fayles,
   to guide his will;
He into mischiefe,
   runneth headlong still.

Most people takes
   Idlenesse, for no sinne :
Thus in Simplicitie,
   Sathan deludes,
That precious time is lost,
   that Grace might winne.

                    End

And want of action,
　　many sinnes includes:
That minde, which vnto
　　Idlenesse giues way,
Doth open lye
　　to bee the Deuils prey.

When DAVID vnto ease
　　himselfe had giuen,
His eyes extrauagantly
　　looke about,
VRIAH's wife he spyeth
　　in the Euen,
He must, and did enioy her
　　without doubt :
Sathan by this his fall
　　more strength doth gaine,
For DAVID bids
　　VRIAH should be slaine.

Thus

Thus by one meanes or other
        Sathan snares
Mans soule in Sinne,
        and hudwinck'd tills him on;
His cup of Gold
        is filled vp with teares
A bitter pittance
        to theyr sweetes belong :
Pride, in it selfe
        doth beare a poyson'd breath,
No Sinne so small
        but punisht is with Death.

That sinn's thought least
        that's spent in trimming fine
That Carkasse vilde,
or which the Wormes must prey,
They thinke not how
        theyr hungry Soule doth pine,
                                They

They count not
of theyr reckoning at last day.
But time of Grace, once lost,
is without call,
So headlong to destruction
they doe fall.

Pride, of all other
sembleth most the Divell?
'Twas Pride, threw Sathan
downe from Heaven to Hell:
'Twas Pride, that Author was
of all mans euill:
'Twas Pride, made Eue
desire still to excell;
When Sathan said,
as Gods, you then shall be;
Incontinent, she tasted
of that Tree.

This

This Lep'rous sinne,
    infected so the bloud,
That through her off-spring,
    it hath wholly runne ;
Before the child can know,
    the bad from good ;
It straight is proud,
    Nature, this hurt hath done.
A female sinne,
    it counted was to be,
But now Hermophrodite,
    proved is shee.

Like IVDAS, *Sathan*
    with each mortall deales,
His haile, is Hate,
    his flattering kisse, is death,
He every where
    still watching, creeping steales,
        With

With armed troupes
    to stifle his soules breath :
His Syrens songs,
   mans mortall Death intends,
And hee must Dye
  that thereto his eare lends.

As a Physition
   with his Patient still
Applyes his potion
   as he findes it fit ,
Giuing to some, more strong
   because theyr ill
Disposed body,
   oft requireth it :
Euen so, doth Sathan
   with each Creature deale,
But his is meant for death
   and not to heale.

                     Nature

Nature and Sathan,
   are sworne Brothers still,
For neyther of them
   moveth man to good;
By Nature, we incline
   to all that's ill,
Which runneth through
   our body with our blood:
And by our Nature
   oft he vs assailes,
And through our weaknesse
   he oft times prevailes.

He, by our Nature sees
   to what we bend,
Whether to goodnesse
   or to mischiefes run;
And if he find man ayme
   at the best end,

          Then

Then strives he for to marre
   all he hath done,
And by a pride of Goodnes
   makes him be,
Towards his God,
    like the proud Pharisie.

The blessings, God to man
   doth often giue,
As beautie, health, riches,
   honours and fame,
That he, in thankefulnes
   for them should: liue,
Still vsing them
   to glorifie his Name :
Sathan transeformeth
   all this vnto sinne,
Through vilde abuse,
   or confidence therein.

             This

This thing, the Scripture
   euidently showes,
By DAVIDS numbering
   of Israell,
Whereby he thought
   more trust for to repose
In his great army,
   this to sinne befell:
And drawing on
   Gods Iudgement for the same,
A heavy plague
   he on his Realme did gaine.

There is a sinne, on which
   small count is made,
And that is Disobedience;
   for which sinne,
SAMVEL the Prophet
   vnto SAVL once sayd;

From

From being King
    God had reiected him:
When as he AMELECK
    all should have slaine,
Sathan mov'd him
    to let the best remaine.

This sinne, so great
    in Gods pure sight doth seeme,
As that the Prophet
    plainly doth him tell:
The Lord no better
    of it doth esteeme;
Then, of wild Witchcraft
    which in Israel,
The Lord commanded
    banish'd quite to be;
This, like to that
    and to Idolatrie.

                              This

This onely sinne
  on all Mankinde did draw,
Gods heavy wrath,
  for this, we suffer still.
By ADAMS *breaking*
  Gods commanded Law;
Sinne with a poysned dart
  our soules did kill:
For through the breach thereof
  there entred death,
For so 'twas sentenced
  by Gods owne breath.

O this same sinne,
  as an accusing one
On all occasions
  still it guilty sayth:
Fulfill Gods Law, who did
  nere yet, was knowne,

     But

But CHRIST who came
   for to appeaſe Gods wrath:
Then by his Law
   we all convicted ſtand,
And howerly may
   looke for Gods wrath at hand.

Deferring off Repentance
   is a bayte
So cloſely layd
   by that old Enemy,
That few doth diue
   the depth of his deceit,
But vnprouided
   many men doe die:
He bids them on the good theeſe
   their eyes caſt,
Who neuer did, repent him
   till the laſt.

               Oſſt,

O flye, deceitfull
    cruell enemy,
How deadly, is thy hatred
    to vs all
Thou EHVD like
    hides that will cause vs dye,
And sith thou fell'st
    thou aym'st still at our fall :
In Paradice the Tree
    death did vs give,
But by the Tree
    in Golgotha, we live.

From a decline in goodnesse
    let each Soule,
With heedfull care
    still study to beware ;
Least in the end
    for it he doth condole,

        I   When

When as his foote
    is fettered in the snare :
Who once his hand
    vpon the Plough doth lay,
Must by no meanes
    looke backe another way.

Easie it is, to plunge
    our selues in sinne,
But, O alas !
    hard to get forth againe ;
If by our faults
    our Soules be black with in,
We then shall finde
    all his delusions vaine;
His voyce of peace
    all peace doth from vs take,
Then shun that hearbe
    where vnder lyes the Snake.

                     Mat

Man ought at all times
      have a carefull eye;
For many are the Snares
      which Sathan layes :
When least he thinketh on
      to cause him dye,
He hides the bayte
   the which mans soule betrayes.
Of ease and pleasures
      he will alwayes tell,
But his smooth path
      the brode way is to Hell.

Who on this Panthers skinne
      doth gazing stand,
Had need beware
      who lyes in wayte to catch,
Who holdes a Woolfe by th'eares
      but with one hand,

                              Must

Must with the other
    muzzell vp his chaps :
If better thou dost get
    leaue not off so,
But of all meanes to hurt,
    depriue thy Foe.

That man, the which
    his Enemy foyl'd hath,
Must straight vnarme him
    least he gather strength ;
BENHADADS seruants
    after AHABS wrath,
With feyned words
    did come to him at length :
And from his kindnesse
    they aduantage draw,
For he, that fear'd to dye
    now made a Law.

                      By

By his Example
    let vs warned bee,
Gods Prophet vnto AHAB
    ſtraight doth come,
And ſayd, Becauſe from death
    thou didſt him free,
Be ſure thy life ſhall ſtand
    in his lifes roome.
Leave thou not Sathan,
    till thou ſeeſt him dead,
And IAEL *like,*
    kill SISERA *in the head.*

He aymes not at thy ſlips,
    but overthrow ;
Small hurts content him not,
    he life would ſpill :
With ſlight advantages,
    he will not goe :

When

When thou *securest* art,
   he waites to kill :
And I O A B like
   of thy health he'll inquire,
But 'tis not life,
   but death he doth desire.

Can this old Serpent,
   this deceiuing Diuell,
Get in his head,
   then follow shall his tayle,
If man but yeeld a little,
   vnto euill,
Sinne will increase,
   though creeping like a Snaile.
And if vnto a Custome,
   it doth'come,
He feeles it not,
   his soule is now growne num.
        All

All Sathan baites,
　　are glittering to the eye,
He leades man on,
　　in a delightsome traine :
Till death arrests them,
　　saying thou must dye,
And then he lets them see
　　all was but vaine :
Then in the ugli'st forme
　　hee shewes them all,
That into Desperation
　　man may fall.

Now having such a strong
　　and powerfull foe,
What need hath Man
　　with heedfull care to watch,
Least on a suddaine
　　he from hence doe goe,

I 4　　　　　For

For Death *as well*
　　doth lye in wayt to catch :
Who proves a welcome guest
　　to a good man,
For unprovided, come
　　he never can.

Deaths ghastly lookes
　　to a god man seemes sweet,
Who still prepared hath
　　for that his end ;
As ESAV IACOB, *did*
　　embracing meet,
So doth he death
　　accounting him his friend :
If teares doe fall
　　they are not shed through feares
For ioy he's come
　　forceth from him those teares.
　　　　　　　　　Can

Can he expect Death
   Enemie to be,
Who by his Prefent
   hath his force alayd:
He fent before good workes,
   much Charity,
Bleſſings of Orphants
   which for him have pray'd:
His ſighs and teares,
   appeafed hath his King,
And this ſuppeſed Fce
   glad newes doth bring.

Death is a true guide
   to Eternall bliſſe,
Portall of Heaven,
   by which we enter muſt,
The Ladder reaching
   to true happineſſe,

I 5   *Which*

Which bringeth man
    to live amongst the Iust :
By him we come .
    Gods glorious face to see,
From which by life
    depriu'd we still shall bee.

Our flesh a prison is
    vnto our soule,
Which doth deprive it
    of that heavenly light ;
With spirituall groanes & sighs
    it doth condole,
Till it attaine
    vnto that wished sight :
Death is the key
    vnlocks our misery,
Looseth our bonds
    and gives vs liberty.

                Deaths

Death's fangs are par'd
    his bitter potions sweet,
His edge abaited
    all his hurt is done,
A godly man
    most kindly he doth meete,
And of a Foe
    he is a Friend become:
His strooke is like
    the striking of a veine,
By which small smart
sick men theyr health doe gaine:

Death is the ending
    of our dayes, not life,
For having clos'd these eyes
    we wake to live,
Death having finisht
    once this mortall strife;

Our

Our Faith in CHRIST
        new life to vs doth give :
Our Night is past
        our Day-star doth appeare,
Our Cloud is vanish'd
        and our Morne shines cleare.

Now ends all sorrowes,
        now all griefes are done,
Sinne takes his leave
        and weaknesse hath his end;
And now behold
        our Iubilee is come,
The Haruest of our labors
        we attend :
Death's potion onely
        bitter is in show;
The taste once past
        no operation so.

MANS

Mans Glaße once run
    his flower of Life once dead,
That vapor vanish'd
    and that span once graß'd,
His breath once failing
    all his body's Lead,
In senceleße, coldneße
    all his parts are claß'd:
He came from earth,   (gives.
    earth house-roome now him
His spirit from God
    with God for ever lives.

The carnall wicked
    worldly minded men,
Who in this life
    their whole content have plac'd
Doth tremble, when Death
    mention'd is to them,
                Because

Because by him
   all Ioyes from them are chased:
Their ease and pleasures
   changed quite will be,
All mirth is dash'd
   by present miserie.

The sight of him
   vnto their mindes doe bring
Remembrance of their sinnes
   they slightly past,
The which with woe
   their soules doe sorely sting :
For that they see
     the count call'd on at last :
Which sure on earth
   a hell may deemed be,
When without mercy
   man his sinnes doth see.
            Those

Those men which onely
   to delights are given,
At the approach of death
   doth feare and quake,
What earth afforded
   they accounted heaven,
And now perforce
   they must those ioyes forsake,
Gods blessings they
   most wildly have abus'd,
And proffered time of Grace,
   they have refus'd.

And now those words
   which ABRAHAM did say,
To DIVES, when for water
   he did call;
He findes too true
   whose smarts without alay,

His

His Sorrowes farre more bitter
      are then gaule:
His good things onely
         were upon this Earth,
But life and them, are parted
      quite by death.

Terrors and feares
   must needs their soules affright,
When guilty Conscience
         showes Gods angry eye,
O how they tremble!
      to approach that sight,
To whom their sinne
      will out for vengeance cry;
He who on earth
      to grieve, they did not feare,
Will give a sentence
      which their Soules will teare.

                                    O

O how mans sinnes
   that mild aspect doth change,
He, which for man did bleed
   doth man condemne,
If by their sinnes
   from the right path they range,
Wanting their guide
   dangers approacheth them :
The Woolfe once seazing
   'tis in vaine to flye,
Theyr Shepheard heares not
   bootlesse 'tis to cry.

Alas, who would this world
   as ought esteeme,
If truely he consider
   every thing,
Those pleasures which to man
   most happy seeme,
           Doth

Doth sooneſt fade
  and gone they leave a ſting :
Man vpon Earth
  no ſure abiding hath,
Then feare betime
  before thou feele Gods wrath.

BILSHAZAR when hee was
  carrouſing ſet,
Amongſt his Princes
  in his royall Throne ;
A writing turnes
  thoſe faire delights to let,
A hand then ſhew'd
  makes bone incounter bone,
He fearefull ſits
  whilſt thus it doth indite,
Thou'rt weigh'd in ballance
  and art found too light,

       Mans

Mans life's a *sceane*
  and tragicke wo's succeed,
A Comet *alwayes*
  future harmes foretell,
The happiest life
  by death is made to bleed,
If vnprepar'd he dye
  he goes to hell :
The gate is shut,
  and they must take their lot ,
For 'twill be answered ;
  loe, I know you not.

Vnto a thorney field
  and barren land,
How fitly may mans life
  compared be,
What cares, what feares,
  what griefes, are still at hand,
    And

And for one Ioy
    ten discontents we see:
We alwayes walke
    as on a bridge of glasse,
And oft it crakes
    as ouer it we passe.

Still barren is this world
    of true content,
Fruitfull enough
    in procreating woes,
Thorny afflictions
    towards vs are bent,
But certaine Ioyes
    still backwards from vs goes:
Who thinkes to catch them
    doth a shadow chase,
And like IXION
    doth a cloud embrace

                Then

Then why should man
    thus waste his precious time,
And triflingly let slip
    his golden dayes ;
O ! turne to God,
    whilst thou art in thy prime,
And put not off
    repentance with delayes :
For when death comes
    it then will be too late,
By teares or vowes
    for to prorogue thy state.

Boast not of youth, or honours
    wealth, or strength,
Who trusts to them
    vpon a reede doth leane,
The which be sure
    deceiue thee will at length.
            Then

Then strive from these vaine
   thy selfe to weane, (thoughts
And fill thy Lampe with oyle
   whil'st thou hast space,
Least afterward too late
   thou call for grace.

Breake off thy sinnes
   by true repentant teares,
And turne to God
   whilst it is call'd to day,
And rest assured
   he their prayers heares,
That vnto him
   vncessantly doe pray;
For to incourage thee,
   he this did say,
Who comes to me
   I will not cast away.

Is not mans life
  compared vnto a flower,
And, O how soone! alas,
  the same doth fade and dye,
Then let man liue
  prepar'd (each day and houre)
Least vnawares
  the force of death he try:
And beare this saying
  alwayes in thy minde,
As death, thee leaues
  so iudgement will thee find.

And as the Flower
  in the chiefest prime,
Doth fade and dye
  when Sun his face doth hide,
For 'tis not in the earth's
  vast slippery clime,

      An

An euer fading beeing
   to prouide :
No more can strength
   or skill preuaile at all,
To lengthen life
   when God by death doth call.

And as the spring
   the water forth doth put,
And by the earth drunke vp
   no more is seene,
So when by death
   our thrid of life is cut,
On earth we are
   as we had neuer beene:
Then whil'st we liue
   let's striue to purchase Grace,
That after Death
   in Heaven we may have place.
            Alas !

Alas ! how many are
    the snares and bayts,
Which Sathan layes,
    our poore soules to betray,
HIENA like,
    he murthers by deceites,
Through false delights
    to cause us misse our way,
His Mermaides Songs
    are onely sweet in sound,
Approach them not,
    lest Death thy life doth wound.

Therefore the safest way
    vnto our blisse,
Is meditation
    of our certaine Death
And though we tread
    the steps of carefulnesse,

K   And

*And all our life
    in sorrow draw our breath,
The guerdon of our paines
        our* CHRIST *will give
In causing vs
        eternally to live.*

*Thus by a godly
        and an vpright life,
Man of a deadly foe
        may make a friend
And by a wise prouision
        stint that strife,
Which Sathan laid
        to bring vs to our end:
And though our flesh
        proue false, our God is Iust,
By death our soule
        gaines heauen, our body dust.*

Be

Be ever vigilant
    in all thy wayes,
And alwayes live
    as in the sight of God,
Performe good actions
    and use no delayes,
Then feare not Death
    it brings with it no rod:
With care attend
    that sure uncertainety,
And live, as every howre
    thou shouldest dye.

This watchfull care
    wounds Sathan in the head,
For hee that thinkes of Death
    doth shun all Sinne,
By thought of this
    man to the world proves dead

K 2   Hee

He counts all droſſe
    and only CHRIST *would win:*
No earthly Ioyes
        can cauſe him life to love,
His Soule is fixt
        and nothing can him move.

Thus each weake Chriſtian
        may this tyrant foyle,
For by CHRIST's *Death*
        man armed is with ſtrength,
Though in this Combate
        he a while may toyle,
But Faith in CHRIST,
        gives victory at length ;
And with a courage bold,
        man now may cry
Death where's thy ſting ?
        Grave where's thy victory ?
                        What

What though we dye,
    as dye we surely must,
Yet by this death,
    we now are gainers made.
For when our bodyes
    are consum'd to dust,
We shall be rais'd,
    from that Eternall shade :
Our mortall bodyes,
    shall immortall be,
And with our Soules,
    inioy Eternitie.

Our troubles in this life,
    now changed are ;
From tokens of his wrath,
    unto his love.
For though a while
    vpon the Earth we share ;

Of

Of griefes and troubles,
 yet when God above:
Shall by death call vs
 from the vaile of sinne,
Wee shall inioy
  Eternall blisse with him.

Where all teares shall
 be wiped from our eyes,
All griefes and sorrowes
 then shall ended be,
We shall be freed
 from all clamarous cries,
No discontents nor troubles
 shall wee see :
But Peace, and Ioyes,
 and comforts shall be found,
And alwayes in our eares
 a heavenly sound.

     Our

Our Sences shall partake
    all of this Blisse,
Our Eyes shall evermore
    behold our King,
Our Hearing heavenly musicke
    shall possesse,
Our Tongues shall evermore
    his Praises sing :
Thus Smell, and Taste,
  thus hands, and eares, and sight,
Shall evermore inioy
    a full delight.

Vnto this Happinesse
    and place of Ioy,
In thy good time
  sweet Saviour Christ vs bring,
Where being freed
    from Sorrowes and annoy,
            VVee

Wee evermore
        thy blessed Praise may sing :
Where we shall never cease
        but Night and Day,
Sing Praise and Glory,
        unto Thee alway.

FINIS.